Franz Ahn

A new, practical, and easy method of learning the German language

Franz Ahn

A new, practical, and easy method of learning the German language

ISBN/EAN: 9783744605816

Hergestellt in Europa, USA, Kanada, Australien, Japan

Cover: Foto ©Andreas Hilbeck / pixelio.de

Weitere Bücher finden Sie auf **www.hansebooks.com**

A NEW, PRACTICAL AND EASY METHOD OF LEARNING THE GERMAN LANGUAGE.

BY

F. AHN.

FIRST COURSE.

TWENTY-EIGHTH EDITION.

LEIPZIG:
F. A. BROCKHAUS.
—
1872.

All Rights reserved.

PREFACE.

Learn a foreign language as you learned your mother tongue, this is in a few words the method which I have adopted in this little work. It is the way that nature herself follows; it is the same which the mother points out to us in speaking to her child, repeating to him a hundred times the same words; combining them imperceptibly and succeeding in this way to make him speak the same language she speaks. To learn in this manner is no longer a study, it is an amusement.

Supposing the pupil to have learned his own language by principles, I thought it proper to add a few rules, which will serve to shorten the course and render the progress more secure.

The Author.

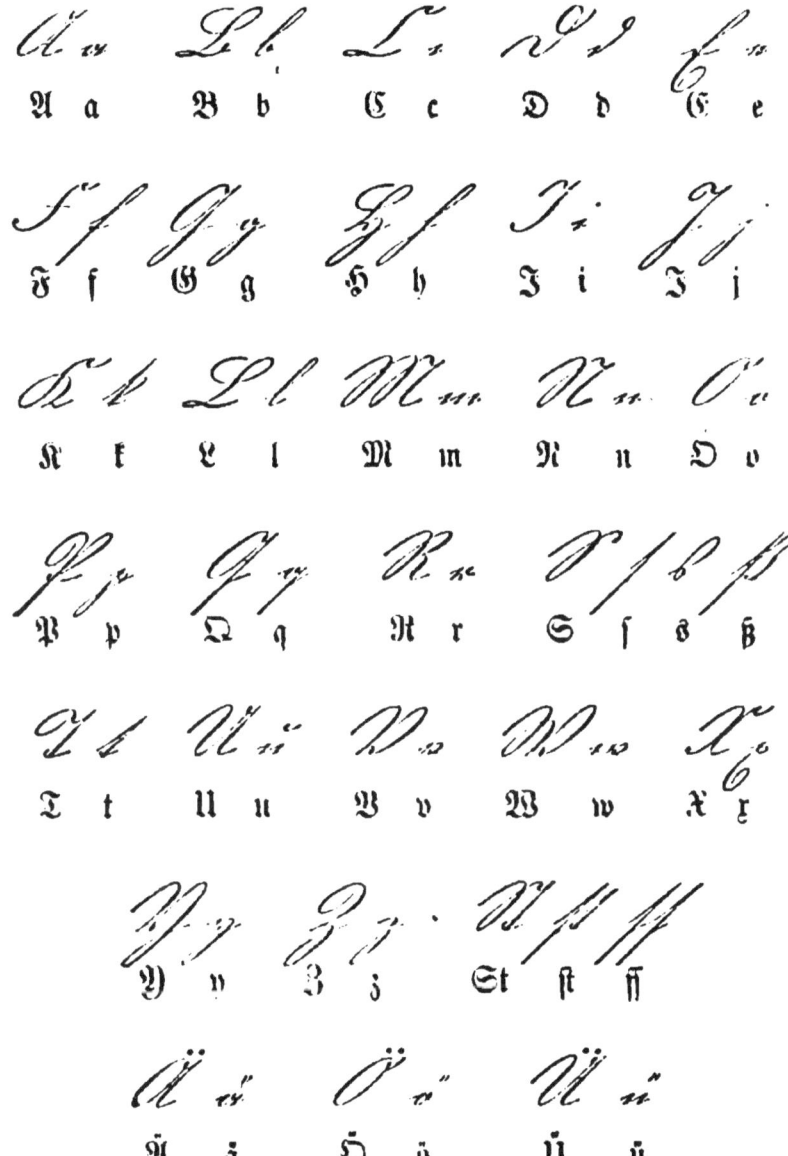

The Pronunciation.

I. *The Alphabet.*

The German Alphabet is composed of the following twenty-six letters:

U,	a,	a.	N,	n,	n.
B,	b,	b.	D,	o,	o.
C,	c,	c.	P,	p,	p.
D,	d,	d.	Q,	q,	q.
E,	e,	e.	R,	r,	r.
F,	f,	f.	S,	ſ, ß,	s.
G,	g,	g.	T,	t,	t.
H,	h,	h.	U,	u,	u.
I,	i,	i.	V,	v,	v.
J,	j,	j.	W,	w,	w.
K,	k,	k.	X,	x,	x.
L,	l,	l.	Y,	y,	y.
M,	m,	m.	Z,	z,	z.

The vowels are: a, ä, e, i, o, ö, u, ü. The diphthongs or compound vowels are: ai, ei, au, äu, eu; all other letters are consonants.

II. *Simple vowels.*

Every vowel, followed by two consonants, is pronounced short; followed by only one consonant, it is long.

A, a, is pronounced like *a* in the English word *father*.

   Alter,   banken,   Frage,
   Vater,   laben,   Galle.

Ä, ä, is pronounced like *a* in the English word *care*.

   Kälte,   Lärm,   Blätter,
   Käse,   Säbel,   Länder.

E, e, is pronounced like *e* in the English word *letter.*

    Esel,   denken,   Titel,
    Ekel,   trennen,   Männer,
    reden,   Ende,   Rebe.

I, i, is pronounced like *e* in the English word *me*.

    Iltis,   immer,   in,
    finden,   Silber,   Kind.

O, o, is pronounced like *o* in the English word *hope*.

    Ofen,   sondern,   Kost,
    rollen   oder,   Wort.

Ö, ö, is pronounced like *u* in the English word *murder.*

    Böse,   tönen,   Löffel,
    Löwe,   können,   Dörfer.

U, u, is pronounced like *oo* in the English word *roof*.

    Blut,   Bruder,   Mund,
    Blume,   Mutter,   Stunde.

Ü, ü, is pronounced like the French *u*. There is no corresponding sound in the English language.

    üben,   müde,   Mütter,
    trübe,   prüfen,   Nüsse.

Y, y, has the sound of the German *i*, by which it is generally replaced.

III. *Double vowels.*

The double vowels aa, ee, oo, are no diphthongs, because only one letter is sounded, and the second only serves to indicate that the syllable is long.

    Aar,   Meer,   Moos,
    Saal,   Seele,   Boot.

Je, ie, is pronounced like *ea* in the English word *meat.*

    Biene,   Bier,   tief,
    lieben,   Dieb,   Lieb.

IV. *Diphthongs.*

In the German diphthongs, the two vowels must be sounded one after the other, but so quickly as to form only one syllable.

Ai and ei are pronounced almost alike, and have the sound of the English *i* in the word *fire.*

Saite, Kaiſer, leiben,
Seite, reimen, Wein.

Au, is pronounced like *ou* in the English word *house*.

Maus, rauben, blau,
Baum, laufen, kaum.

Äu and **eu**, are both pronounced like *oy* in the English word *joy*.

Mäuſe, Beutel, Freund,
Bäume, Feuer, Treue.

V. *Consonants.*

The pronunciation of the consonants differs but little in the two languages; the scholar should remark the following peculiarities.

C, c, before ä, e, and i, is pronounced like *ts*.

Cäſar, Ceder, Citrone.

Before a, o, u, before a consonant and at the end of a syllable it is pronounced like *k*, by which in most cases it may be replaced.

Carl, Curt, Tombac,
Conrad, Creole, Claſſe.

Ch, at the beginning of a word is pronounced like *k*, except in words derived from the French, when it preserves the French pronunciation.

Chor, Charlatan,
Chriſt, Charivari.

In the middle or at the end of a word ch has a pronunciation quite peculiar to the German language, and more or less guttural, but for which no corresponding sound can be found in English; it is like the Scotch *ch* in the word *loch* after a, o, u, au, but softer after ä, e, i, ö, ü, äu, eu, and after a consonant.

Dach, Rauch, nichts,
Loch, Küche, rechnen,
Buch, Kirche, ſuchen,
Licht, Tochter, Bäumchen.

chs or **chſ** is pronounced like *x* when these consonants belong to the root or radical syllable.

Wachs, Fuchs, wachſen,
Ochs, ſechs, Büchſe.

But the ch preserves its guttural pronunciation,

when it stands before the ⸗s or ⸗j by contraction or in a composed word.

nachſehen, wachſam, des Buchs instead of des Buches.

G, g, at the beginning of a syllable is pronounced like the English *g* in the word *good;* but between two vowels, in the middle of a word and at the end of a syllable it has a sound like the ch, only much softened.

    gehen,   groß,   Gabe,
    Wagen,   Sieg,   artig,
    Regen,   Krug,   richtig.

After n at the end of a word it is pronounced like a very soft *k*.

    Gang,   Ring,   Sprung.

H, h, is always aspirated at the beginning of a syllable.

    hier,   hart,   Hecht,
    Haus,   Himmel,   Freiheit.

The aspiration becomes however almost imperceptible before an e in the end-syllables.

    Reihe,   Ruhe,   sehen.

After a vowel or a t, the h is not pronounced, but only indicates that the syllable is long.

    Hahn,   Stroh,   Thier,
    Mehl,   Reh,   Thür,
    Uhr,   früh,   Rath.

J, j, only stands at the beginning of a syllable, and is pronounced like the English *y* in the word *yet*.

    Jahr,   Joch,   Jugend.

ck replaces the double *k*, and is pronounced short.

    Stock,   Brücke,   Acker.

Qu, qu, has the sound of *qu* in English.

    Qual,   Quelle,   Quer.

S, ſ, s, at the beginning of a syllable is pronounced like the English *z*, at the end of a syllable however like the English *s*.

    Sommer,   Reise,   Haus,
    Sack,   Eisen,   Reis.

The long ſ is placed at the beginning and in the middle, s only at the end of syllables. If in a non-composed word there are two ſ one after another, they are written ſſ.

    Waſſer,   wiſſen,   müſſen.

ß is only placed at the end or in the middle of

syllables; it is always preceded by a long vowel, and has the sound of the English *ss*.

        Straße,   groß,   fließen.

Sch, sch is pronounced like the English *sh*.

        Schatten,   Schule,   Peitsche,
        schlafen,   Schilt,   Tisch.

st and **sp** are pronounced like *st* and *sp* in English; but in some parts of Germany they pronounce st at the beginning of a word like *sht*, and sp like *shp*.

        Stuhl,   stehlen,   spielen,
        Stern,   sprechen,   stechen.

V, v, has the sound of *f*.

        Vater,   Vogel,   Vieh.

W, w, is pronounced like the English *v*.

        Welt,   Wiese,   Wand.

Z, z, is sounded like *ts*.

        Zahl,   Zorn,   Holz,
        Zeit,   zwanzig,   Herz.

ß replaces the double z and is pronounced very hard.

        Blitz,   Nutzen,   setzen.

VI. *Syllabic Accent.*

The Germans never pronounce several successive syllables one after the other with the same force; the principal syllables are pronounced with a louder and the others with a softer tone. The end-syllables in German words are pronounced very softly.

The accent is always laid upon the radical syllable, that is, upon the one which includes the principal idea: thus in the word Gerechtigkeit (justice) which is derived from recht (just), the second syllable is pronounced more strongly than the rest.

In compound words, the first syllable always has the accent, because it presents the principal idea and modifies the following one: Blumengarten, Gartenblume.

Part I.

1.

Singular. ich bin, I am;
du bist, thou art;
er ist, he is;
sie ist, she is;
Plural. wir sind, we are;
ihr seid, you are;
sie sind, they are.

Gut, good; groß, great, large, big; klein, little, small; reich, rich; arm, poor; jung, young; alt, old; müde, tired; krank, ill, sick.

Ich bin groß. Du bist klein. Er ist alt. Sie ist gut. Wir sind jung. Ihr seid reich. Sie sind arm. Bin ich groß? Bist du müde? Ist er krank? Ist sie jung? Sind wir reich? Seid ihr arm? Sind sie alt?

2.

I am little. Thou art young. We are tired. They are rich. Art thou sick? You are poor. Is she old? Are you sick? Are they good? He is tall (groß). Am I poor?

3.

Nicht, not.

Stark, strong; treu, faithful; faul, idle, lazy; fleißig, diligent; böse, wicked, naughty; traurig, sad; glücklich, happy; höflich, polite.

Bist du böse? Ich bin nicht böse. Er ist traurig. Wir sind nicht stark. Sind sie treu? Bist du nicht glücklich? Ihr seid nicht fleißig. Sie ist nicht faul. Ist er nicht müde? Wir sind nicht arm. Sind sie nicht höflich? Du bist nicht krank.

4.

I am not tall. They are idle. She is not ill. We are not happy. He is not short (klein). Are you not tired? They are not rich. Is he not diligent? Thou art not strong. They are not happy. He is not polite. Are they not faithful? Is she not rich? He is not wicked.

5.

Masculine nouns: der Vater, the father; der Garten, the garden.
Feminine nouns: die Mutter, the mother; die Stadt, the town.
Neuter nouns: das Kind, the child; das Haus, the house.
Schön, beautiful, fine; lang, long; hoch, high; neu, new; und, and; sehr, very.

Der Vater ist gut. Die Mutter ist traurig. Das Kind ist faul. Der Garten ist nicht sehr lang. Die Stadt ist groß und reich. Das Haus ist nicht hoch. Ist der Garten schön? Ist der Vater krank? Ist das Kind nicht fleißig? Ist das Haus neu? Der Vater und die Mutter sind glücklich.

Observation. All German substantives begin with a capital letter. — When two or more substantives follow each other, the article must be repeated before each, unless they are all of the same gender.

6.

The house is not new. The mother and (the) child are ill. The town is very beautiful. The child is not naughty. The father is very old. The house and (the) garden are very large. Is the mother not happy? The house is not very old. Is the garden not very fine? The house is very small.

7.

Masc. dieser Baum, this tree.
Fem. diese Frau, this woman.
Neut. dieses Pferd, this horse.

Der Mann, the man; der Berg, the mountain; die Blume, the flower; das Fenster, the window; offen, open; zufrieden, contented, satisfied, pleased; oder, or.

Dieser Mann ist sehr arm. Dieses Fenster ist sehr hoch. Diese Blume ist schön. Dieses Pferd ist jung und stark. Ist diese Frau glücklich? Dieser Vater und diese Mutter sind nicht zufrieden. Dieser Baum ist sehr groß. Diese Frau ist arm und krank. Dieses Kind ist sehr böse. Dieser Mann ist nicht höflich. Bist du traurig oder krank?

8.

This woman is tired. This mountain is not high. Is this child good or naughty? This man is not satisfied.

This child is not very diligent. Is this garden small or large? Art thou not contented? This window is not open. Is this house old or new? This tree is very fine. Is this man rich or poor? This town is very dull (traurig).

9.

Masc.	*Fem.*	*Neut.*	
Ein,	eine,	ein,	a;
mein,	meine,	mein,	my;
dein,	deine,	dein,	thy.

Der Bruder, the brother; die Schwester, the sister; die Feder, the pen; das Buch, the book; der Freund, the friend; Karl, Charles; Luise, Louisa; wo, where; hier, here; noch, still, yet; aber, but.

Mein Bruder ist traurig. Meine Schwester ist krank. Mein Buch ist schön. Ist dein Garten groß? Ist deine Feder gut? Ist dein Pferd klein? Karl ist noch ein Kind. Berlin ist eine Stadt. Luise ist meine Schwester. Dein Bruder ist mein Freund. Dein Vater ist nicht hier. Wo ist mein Buch? Ist mein Buch nicht hier? Ist deine Mutter noch krank? Ich bin noch nicht müde, aber dein Bruder und deine Schwester sind sehr müde.

10.

Charles is my brother. This child is my sister. Thou art my friend. Thy garden is very large. Where is thy mother? A friend is faithful. Is this child thy brother? This horse is still young. Where is my pen? Thy pen is here. Louisa is still a child. Thy brother is idle. My friend is very diligent.

11.

Masc.	*Fem.*	*Neut.*	
Unser,	unsere,	unser,	our;
euer,	euere,	euer,	your;
ihr,	ihre,	ihr,	their.

Der Sohn, the son; die Tochter, the daughter; die Thüre, the door; immer, always.

Obs. In addressing any one, the third person plural is from politeness used instead of the second: Sie sind, instead of ihr seid. For the same reason Ihr is used instead of euer. In this case the pronoun is always written with a capital letter.

Unser Garten ist groß. Unsere Mutter ist krank. Unser Pferd ist schön. Dieser Mann ist unser Vater. Diese Frau ist unsere Mutter. Karl ist euer Bruder. Luise ist eure Schwester. Ist Ihr Sohn fleißig? Ist Ihre Tochter zufrieden? Wo ist Ihr Buch? Unser Haus ist alt. Unsere

Thüre ist immer offen. Dieser Vater und diese Mutter sind sehr traurig; ihr Sohn ist immer krank.

12.

Our father is good. Our mother is little. Our child is ill. Is this man your brother? Is this woman your mother? Your son is not always diligent. Is your horse beautiful? This child is our brother. Is Charles not your friend? Louisa is not your sister.

13.

Klein, little, small:	kleiner, smaller;
alt, old;	älter, older;
groß, great;	größer, greater;
jung, young;	jünger, younger;
fleißig, diligent;	fleißiger, more diligent.

Nützlich, useful; unglücklich, unhappy; der Hund, the dog; die Katze, the cat; die Sonne, the sun; der Mond, the moon; als, than, as.

Obs. In forming the Comparative of an adjective, the radical vowel a generally changes into ä; o into ö; and u into ü.

Mein Bruder ist älter als ich. Ich bin jünger als mein Freund. Karl ist größer als Luise. Dieser Mann ist größer als wir. Der Hund ist treuer als die Katze. Das Pferd ist schöner und nützlicher als der Hund. Dieses Kind ist fleißiger als du. Sie sind glücklicher als Ihr Bruder. Karl ist stärker als ich. Wir sind zufriedener als ihr. Luise ist höflicher als deine Schwester. Ist dein Bruder jünger, als du? Er ist älter, aber kleiner als ich.

14.

My brother is more diligent than thou. Thou art not younger than he. He is taller and stronger than I. Your son is younger than this child. The moon is smaller than the sun. Art thou older than I? This dog is finer than this cat. Your sister is politer than you. I am more contented than thou. You are richer than we. We are more unhappy than you.

15.

Gut, good;	besser, better;
hoch, high;	höher, higher;
dieser, diese, dieses, this, this one;	
jener, jene, jenes, that, that one.	

Das Eisen, the iron; das Blei, the lead; der Stahl, the steel; die Erde, the earth; schwer, heavy; hart, hard; theuer, dear; so, so, as; zu, too.

Mein Buch ist schöner als jenes. Meine Feder ist besser als diese. Der Stahl ist härter als das Eisen. Dieser Berg ist höher als jener. Die Katze ist nicht so treu als der Hund. Das Blei ist nicht so hart als das Eisen. Ist Ihr Haus nicht größer als jenes? Ist das Blei theurer als das Eisen? Der Mond ist nicht so groß als die Erde. Dieses Kind ist fleißiger als jenes. Jene Frau ist ärmer als diese. Unser Garten ist nicht so lang und schön als dieser.

16.

(The) lead is heavier than (the) iron. This tree is not so high as that. Is this book not better than that? Our garden is smaller than this one. This house is higher than that one. (The) iron is more useful than (the) lead. I am not so old as he. (The) lead is not so dear as (the) steel. Our town is larger and finer than this one. We are not so rich as this man, but we are more contented than he.

17.

Singular. ich habe, I have;
du hast, thou hast;
er, sie hat, he or she has;
Plural. wir haben, we have;
ihr habt, Sie haben, you have;
sie haben, they have.

Die Uhr, the watch; das Messer, the knife; Recht, right; Unrecht, wrong; Heinrich, Henry; Ludwig, Lewis; für, for; auch, also; warum, why

Obs. The Accusative of the fem. and neut. nouns is like the Nominative. — In German the verb *to have* is used with *right* and *wrong*; thus: ich habe Recht, er hat Unrecht.

Ich habe Recht. Du hast Unrecht. Ich habe ein Buch. Du hast eine Feder. Mein Bruder hat eine Uhr. Wir haben ein Haus. Ihr habt ein Pferd. Karl und Luise haben eine Katze. Hast du eine Schwester? Hat dieser Mann eine Tochter? Habt ihr ein Kind? Diese Uhr ist für meine Mutter. Diese Feder ist für Karl. Haben Sie noch Ihre Mutter? Warum hast du mein Messer? Ich habe dein Messer nicht.

18.

Charles, hast thou my pen? Louisa, hast thou my book? Henry has thy pen, and Lewis has thy book. Thou art right. My son is wrong. We have a book and a pen. Have you also a horse and a watch? This knife is for Henry. Is this watch for thy mother?

Has your friend a knife? Charles and Lewis have a horse. Has your father still a sister? Is this flower for my daughter?

19.

Geſehen, seen; verloren, lost; gefunden, found; gekauft, bought; verkauft, sold; genommen, taken.

Obs. The past participle is detached from the auxiliary and placed at the end of the sentence.

Ich habe mein Buch verloren. Haſt du mein Meſſer gefunden? Ich habe dein Meſſer nicht gefunden. Wo iſt meine Feder? Habt ihr meine Feder? Wir haben deine Feder nicht. Mein Vater hat dieſes Pferd gekauft. Wir haben unſer Haus verkauft. Wo haſt du meine Uhr gefunden? Warum haben Sie meine Uhr genommen? Ich habe Ihre Mutter und Ihre Schweſter geſehen. Warum hat Ihr Vater dieſes Haus nicht gekauft? Hat dein Bruder meine Feder genommen? Er hat deine Feder nicht genommen.

20.

Where hast thou found this book? Have you lost your pen? Has your father bought this horse? Why have you sold your watch? Why have you not taken my pen? My brother has found thy knife. We have seen thy mother. I have not yet seen this woman. Charles and Lewis have lost their mother; they are very sad.

21.

Nominative.	Accusative.	
Der Vater,	den Vater,	the father;
dieſer Vater,	dieſen Vater,	this father.

Der König, the king; der Hut, the hat, bonnet; der Stock, the stick, cane; der Brief, the letter; geſchrieben, written; erhalten, received, got; oft, often; ſchon, already.

Obs. The subject is placed in the nominative case, and the object in the accusative case.

Ich habe den König geſehen. Haſt du den Brief erhalten? Meine Schweſter hat den Brief nicht geſchrieben. Heinrich hat den Stock verloren. Mein Vater hat dieſen Garten und dieſes Haus gekauft. Wo habt ihr dieſen Hund und dieſe Katze gefunden? Ich habe dieſen Mann ſchon oft geſehen. Warum haben Sie dieſen Hut genommen? Wir haben dieſen Brief gefunden. Hat dein Bruder dieſen Stock verloren?

22.

We have sold the house and the garden. Have you bought this dog and this horse? I have seen the man and woman, the son and daughter. I have not written this letter. Where have you found this book and cane? Has thy brother bought this tree? This letter is for this man. Hast thou lost this hat? Hast thou not taken this book and pen? Hast thou already seen the king? I have not yet seen the king.

23.

Nom. ein Garten, } a garden. *Nom.* mein Hund, } my dog.
Accus. einen Garten, } *Accus.* meinen Hund, }

Der Vogel, the bird; der Stuhl, the chair; der Tisch, the table; der Bleistift, the pencil; der Nachbar, the neighbour.

Mein Bruder ist sehr zufrieden; er hat einen Vogel. Hast du einen Brief erhalten? Ich habe meinen Hut verloren. Haben Sie meinen Hund schon gesehen? Wir haben einen Tisch und einen Stuhl gekauft. Mein Bruder hat deinen Stock genommen. Wo hast du deinen Bleistift gekauft? Wir haben unsern Vater und unsere Mutter verloren. Ich habe Ihren Brief nicht erhalten. Hat dein Bruder unsern Garten und unser Haus schon gesehen? Unser Nachbar hat den König gesehen. Hast du diesen Vogel gekauft oder jenen?

24.

We have lost our dog. This man has lost a son and a daughter. Where have you found my pencil? Have you already seen my brother and mother? I have bought a bonnet for my sister. Our neighbour has found thy knife and cane. Where hast thou bought this table? Thy brother has taken my chair. Have you written a letter? We have found this stick and that one.

25.

Nom. sein, seine, sein, } his, its; ihr, ihre, ihr, } her.
Accus. seinen, seine, sein, } ihren, ihre, ihr, }

Gelesen, read; gekannt, known; der Onkel, the uncle; die Tante, the aunt; der Fingerhut, the thimble; die Scheere, the scissors.

Mein Freund ist traurig; sein Vater und seine Mutter sind krank. Meine Tante ist zufrieden; ihr Sohn und ihre Tochter sind sehr fleißig. Heinrich hat seinen Stock, seine

Uhr und sein Messer verloren. Luise hat ihren Fingerhut, ihre Feder und ihr Buch verloren. Euer Onkel hat sein Haus und seinen Garten verkauft. Diese Frau hat ihren Mann und ihr Kind verloren. Diese Tochter hat einen Brief für ihre Mutter geschrieben. Karl hat seinen Vater nicht gekannt. Die Tante hat deinen und meinen Brief gelesen.

26.

The father has lost his son. This mother has lost her daughter. My uncle has sold his watch. Our aunt has sold her scissors. Henry has found his pencil. Louisa has found her thimble. I have seen this man and his son, this woman and her daughter. My mother has lost her pen and her knife. My brother has taken his hat. I have seen your aunt; has she still her horse? This man is very sad; he has lost his wife (Frau). Charles has written a letter for his father. My aunt has bought this book for her son.

27.

Nom. die Mutter, the mother;   diese Mutter, this mother;
Gen. der Mutter, of the mother; dieser Mutter, of this mother;
Die Magd, the maid-servant; die Königin, the queen; die Nachbarin, the female neighbour; angekommen, arrived; abgereist, departed.

Die Mutter der Königin ist angekommen. Der Vater der Nachbarin ist abgereist. Ich habe den Garten der Tante gesehen. Haben Sie den Bleistift der Schwester gefunden? Diese Frau ist die Schwester der Nachbarin. Dieser Mann ist der Bruder der Magd. Das Kind dieser Frau ist immer krank.

28.

The bonnet of the mother is beautiful. The sister of the queen is not beautiful. Is the father of the servant arrived? Are you the brother of the (female) neighbour? I am the sister of this woman. Hast thou taken the chair of the sister? Have you seen the horse of the aunt? We have known the father of this servant.

29.

Nom. der Vater, the father;   dieser Vater, this father.
Gen. des Vaters, of the father; dieses Vaters, of this father;
Nom. das Kind, the child;   dieses Kind, this child;
Gen. des Kindes, of the child;   dieses Kindes, of this child.

Der Schuhmacher, the shoemaker; der Schneider, the tailor; der Gärtner, the gardener; der Kaufmann, the merchant; der Arzt, the physician; das Zimmer, the room; das Volk, the people.

Obs. All neuter nouns and most masculine nouns take **s** or **es** in the Genitive Singular.

Die Magd des Schneiders ist krank. Der Sohn des Nachbars ist noch sehr jung. Die Blume des Gärtners ist sehr schön. Der Garten des Königs ist sehr groß. Der König ist der Vater des Volkes. Die Frau des Arztes ist immer zufrieden. Ich habe den Garten des Onkels gesehen. Wir haben das Pferd des Kaufmanns gekauft. Hast du den Bleistift des Bruders genommen? Wo ist die Magd des Schuhmachers? Die Thüre des Zimmers ist immer offen. Die Tochter dieses Mannes ist abgereist. Wir haben die Mutter dieses Kindes gekannt. Der Garten dieses Hauses ist klein.

30.

This man is the brother of the gardener. This woman is the sister of the shoemaker. This child is the son of the tailor. The door of the house is not open. I have seen the son and daughter of the physician. We have seen the horse of the merchant. The servant of the neighbour is the sister of this gardener. Why is the door of this room open? We have known the son of this merchant. The dog of the neighbour is faithful. The mother of this child is arrived.

31.

Nom. ein Vater, eine Mutter, ein Kind;
Gen. eines Vaters, einer Mutter, eines Kindes;

Der Regenschirm, the umbrella; das Federmesser, the penknife; gestern, yesterday.

Obs. The pronouns mein, dein, sein, ihr, unser, euer, are declined like ein, eine, ein.

Sind Sie der Sohn eines Arztes? Ich bin der Sohn eines Kaufmanns. Haben Sie das Haus meines Nachbars gekauft? Der Bruder deines Freundes ist gestern angekommen. Wo ist der Regenschirm deines Onkels? Hast du das Zimmer meiner Schwester gesehen? Wir haben den Brief deiner Mutter gelesen. Mein Onkel hat das Haus Ihres Vaters gekauft. Ich habe den Stock Ihres Bruders verloren. Der Garten unsers Nachbars ist sehr groß. Unsere Magd ist die Tochter eures Gärtners. Wo ist der Regenschirm unserer Mutter? Karl hat den Fingerhut seiner Schwester genommen. Luise hat das Federmesser ihrer Tante genommen.

32.

I have found the hat of a child. Are you the servant of my uncle? I am the servant of your tailor. The penknife of thy brother is very good. The pen of thy sister is not good. The house of our aunt is large. Henry has lost the letter of his father. Louisa has found the pen of her brother. Is the garden of our uncle as fine as this one? We have found the hat of your neighbour's son (the hat of the son of your neighbour). Lewis has read the letter of his friend. Louisa has bought a flower for a child of her sister.

33.

Nom. der Bruder, the brother;
Dat. dem Bruder, to the brother;
Nom. das Buch, the book; die Schwester, the sister;
Dat. dem Buche, to the book; der Schwester, to the sister;
Gehört, belongs; geliehen, lent; gegeben, given; geschickt, sent; versprochen, promised; gezeigt, shown; der Freund, the friend; die Freundin, the female friend.

Obs. 1) If the Genitive terminates in es, the Dative takes e, Buches, Buche. 2) The Dative generally precedes the Accusative. 3) In interrogative and negative sentences the English auxiliary verb *to do* is not translated in German.

Dieses Haus gehört dem Onkel meines Nachbars. Jener Garten gehört der Tante meines Freundes. Ich habe dem Vater einen Brief geschrieben. Sie hat der Freundin ihrer Schwester eine Blume gegeben. Karl hat der Schwester sein Federmesser geliehen. Hast du dem Arzte mein Buch geschickt? Ich habe diesem Kinde einen Vogel versprochen. Heinrich hat dieser Frau unsern Regenschirm geliehen. Luise hat diesem Manne unsern Garten gezeigt. Ich habe meine Feder dem Freunde meines Bruders gegeben.

34.

This hat belongs to the gardener. This house belongs to the mother of my friend. I have written to my uncle and aunt. My sister has lent her thimble to the friend (fem.) of your brother. My uncle has sent a watch to the son of your neighbour (fem.). Have you given a chair to this child? Have you lent an umbrella to this woman? Does this garden belong to the king? (belongs this garden etc.) No, it belongs to the sister of the king. We have sold our horse to the friend of our uncle. Does this knife belong to this or to that servant?

35.

Nom. ein Buch, a book;   eine Feder, a pen;
Dat. einem Buche, to a book;   einer Feder, to a pen;

Der Vetter, the cousin; die Base, the female cousin; Amalie, Amelia; der Gärtner, the gardener; die Gärtnerin, the gardener's wife.

Dieser Garten gehört einem Schuhmacher. Dieses Messer gehört einer Magd. Luise hat meinem Vater einen Brief geschrieben. Heinrich hat meiner Mutter eine Blume gegeben. Ich habe Ihrem Onkel mein Pferd geliehen. Sie haben unserer Tante ihr Haus verkauft. Karl hat seinem Freunde ein Buch geschickt. Amalie hat ihrer Freundin einen Fingerhut geliehen. Dieser Mann hat eurer Nachbarin einen Vogel geschickt. Hast du meinem Vater diese Uhr gegeben? Habt ihr unserer Base einen Bleistift geliehen?

36.

I have lent my pen to a friend of my brother's. Hast thou given thy cat to a friend (fem.) of my sister's? We have given the letter to a servant of the physician's. Have you sent this flower to our gardener? This garden belongs to my cousin (masc. and fem.). This umbrella does not belong (belongs not) to your brother. Does this pen belong (belongs this pen) to thy brother or to thy sister? Has Henry written to his father or to his mother? Has Louisa written to her uncle or aunt?

37.

Von, of, from, by.
Of the mother, der Mutter, or von der Mutter;
of the child, des Kindes, or von dem Kinde;
of the father, des Vaters, or von dem Vater,
of this garden, dieses Gartens, or von diesem Garten;
of my sister, meiner Schwester, or von meiner Schwester.

Ich spreche, I speak, or I am speaking; wir sprechen, we speak, we are speaking; wird geliebt, is loved.

Obs. Of is expressed by the Genitive, when *of* relates to a substantive, and by von followed by the Dative, when *of* relates to a verb

Ich habe das Buch des Arztes gesehen. Haben Sie dieses Buch von dem Arzte erhalten? Wir haben den Garten unsers Nachbars gekauft. Haben Sie diesen Garten von Ihrem Nachbar gekauft? Ich habe diese Uhr von meinem Onkel erhalten. Heinrich hat einen Brief von seinem Vater und (von) seiner Mutter erhalten. Ich spreche von dem Könige und der Königin. Wir sprechen von Ihrem Bruder und Ihrer Schwester, von diesem Manne und dieser Frau. Sprechen Sie von meinem Vetter oder meiner Base? Heinrich wird von seinem Vater und seiner Mutter geliebt.

38.

I have received this horse from my friend. I have bought this cat of thy sister. Louisa has got an umbrella from her uncle and a watch from her aunt. I speak of this dog and of this cat, of this bird and of this flower. We are speaking of your cousin (masc. and fem.). Amelia is loved by her uncle and aunt. Our gardener's wife has received a letter from her son and daughter. Henry is the son of this shoemaker and Louisa is the daughter of this tailor.

39.

Schön, beautiful; schöner, more beautiful; der schönste, the most beautiful;
gut, good; besser, better; der beste, the best;
hoch, high; höher, higher; der höchste, the highest.
Das Thier, the animal; der Löwe, the lion; der Tiger, the tiger, das Metall, the metal; das Silber, the silver; das Gold, the gold.

Obs. The Superlative is formed by adding ste or este, and softening the radical vowel.

Die Katze ist nicht so stark als der Hund. Der Löwe ist stärker als der Tiger. Der Löwe ist das stärkste Thier. Mein Nachbar ist reicher als Sie; er ist der reichste Mann der Stadt. Das Gold ist schwerer als das Silber. Das Eisen ist nützlicher als das Silber. Das Eisen ist das nützlichste Metall. Luise ist schöner als Amalie; aber Heinrich ist das schönste Kind. Ludwig ist jünger als du; er ist der jüngste Sohn unsers Nachbars. Karl ist älter als ich; er ist der älteste Sohn meines Onkels. Der Hund ist sehr treu. Der Hund ist das treueste Thier. Dieses Buch ist besser als jenes. Du bist der beste Freund meines Bruders. Das Haus dieses Kaufmannes ist das höchste der Stadt.

40.
It is, es ist; that is, das ist.

This bird is very little; it is the smallest bird. Louisa is very beautiful; she is more beautiful than her sister. (The) silver is not so useful as (the) iron. The tiger is not so strong as the lion. The tailor is the happiest man in the town. Henry is more diligent than Lewis, but Charles is the most diligent. Thy umbrella is very beautiful; the umbrella of my cousin is the most beautiful. You are not so poor as my cousin; he is the poorest man in the town. My chair is too high; this one is higher; but the chair of my mother is the highest. I have given my brother the best pencil and the best pen.

41.
Nom. wer, who?
Dat. wem, to whom?
Acc. wen, whom?

Was, what; etwas, something; nichts, nothing; Jemand, anybody, somebody; Niemand, nobody; hier, here; da, there.

Wer ist da? Es ist der Schneider; es ist Heinrich; ich bin es. Wer ist jener Mann? Es ist der Schuhmacher; es ist der Sohn des Arztes. Wer hat diesen Brief geschrieben? Wem gehört dieser Hund? Er gehört unserm Nachbar. Wem gehört diese Uhr? Sie gehört meiner Schwester. Wem haben Sie den Hut gegeben? Von wem haben Sie diese Blume erhalten? Wen haben Sie gesehen? Was haben Sie verloren? Ich habe nichts verloren. Haben Sie etwas gefunden? Wo ist Ihr Bruder? Er ist nicht hier. Ist Jemand da? Es ist Niemand da. Hat Jemand meine Feder genommen? Niemand hat Ihre Feder genommen.

42.
Who is there? It is my tailor; it is Charles. Who is that woman? It is the wife of the shoemaker; it is the servant of the neighbour. To whom have you lent your knife? To the son of the gardener. To whom has your brother sold his dog? To the sister of my friend. From whom hast thou received this bird? From the father of this girl. What have you bought? I have bought an umbrella for my cousin (fem.). What have you taken? I have taken nothing. Of whom do you speak (sprechen Sie)? I am speaking of nobody. Has anybody read my letter? Nobody has read your letter.

43.

Nom. welcher, welche, welches, wno or which;
Dat. welchem, welcher, welchem, to whom or to which;
Acc. welchen, welche, welches, whom or which;

Der Tischler, the joiner; gemacht, made; ausgegangen, gone out; geweint, cried, wept; in, in; mit, with; bei, with (at the house of).

Obs. The prepositions in, mit, bei govern the Dative.

Welcher Tischler hat diesen Tisch gemacht? Welche Magd hat diesen Brief geschrieben? Welches Kind hat geweint? Welchen Hund haben Sie gekauft? Welche Uhr hast du verloren? Welches Haus hat Ihr Vater verkauft? Von welchem Volke sprechen Sie? Mit welchem Freunde bist du ausgegangen? In welchem Garten hat er den Vogel gefunden? Welche Feder hast du da? Welcher Frau hast du dein Messer gegeben? Welchem Mädchen hast du deinen Fingerhut geliehen? Bei welchem Kaufmann haben Sie diesen Bleistift gekauft? Mit welcher Feder haben Sie diesen Brief geschrieben? Mit wem sind Sie angekommen?

44.

Where is your sister? She is in her garden. Where is your brother? He is with (at the house of) his friend. Is your father gone out? He is gone out with the physician. Which hat have you bought? Which book have you read? Which pen have you taken? Which boy is the most diligent? Which watch is the best? From which gardener hast thou received this flower? At the house of (bei) which woman hast thou bought this bird? In which house have you lost your thimble? With whom is your brother departed? To which man have you lent your umbrella? Which stick have you lost? Which joiner has made this table?

45.

Der Apfel, the apple; die Birne, the pear; gegessen, eaten.

Obs. In those sentences which begin with a relative pronoun, the verb is placed at the end.

Wir haben einen Bruder, welcher sehr groß ist. Ihr habt eine Schwester, welche sehr klein ist. Mein Sohn hat ein Buch, welches sehr nützlich ist. Der Garten, welchen dein Onkel gekauft hat, ist sehr schön. Die Feder, welche mein Vetter gefunden hat, ist sehr gut. Ich habe das Haus gesehen, welches Ihr Vater gekauft hat. Haben Sie den

Fingerhut gefunden, welchen meine Schwester verloren hat? Hast du den Apfel gegessen, welchen du gefunden hast? Ich habe die Birne gegessen, welche ich gekauft habe. Hier ist der Mann, welchem Sie Ihren Brief gegeben haben. Hier ist die Frau, welcher wir unsern Hund verkauft haben. Hier ist der Arzt, von welchem wir so oft sprechen.

46.

Obs. Instead of welcher, etc. may be used der, die, das; for instance: der Garten, den or welchen wir gekauft haben.

I have a dog which is very little. We have a cat which is very fine. My father has bought a house which is very beautiful. Have you seen the umbrella which my mother has bought? Hast thou found the pear which thy brother has lost? We have seen the horse which your uncle has sold. Where is the thimble which you have found? I have taken the pencil which my cousin has bought. Henry has eaten the apple which his brother has received. Have you seen the woman of whom we speak? Have you read the letter which I have written? Have you found the boy to whom this penknife belongs?

47.

Derjenige welcher, he who; diejenige welche, she who; dasjenige welches, that which.

Obs. Instead of derjenige, etc. may also be used der, die, das; for instance: der, welcher.

Derjenige, welcher zufrieden ist, ist reich. Dieser Fingerhut ist besser als derjenige meiner Schwester. Diese Uhr ist kleiner als diejenige deines Bruders. Dieses Haus ist schöner als dasjenige unsers Nachbars. Ich habe meinen Hut verloren und den meines Vetters. Wir haben deine Feder gefunden und die deines Freundes. Heinrich hat mein Zimmer gesehen und das meines Onkels. Hast du meinen Stock genommen oder den meines Bruders? Das ist nicht deine Blume, das ist die meiner Mutter. Haben Sie mein Messer oder das des Gärtners? Sprechen Sie von meinem Sohne oder von dem des Arztes? Das Pferd, welches wir gekauft haben, ist jünger, als dasjenige Ihres Vaters.

48.

He who is rich, is not always contented. My dog si more faithful than that of my uncle. Our servant is stronger than that of our neighbour. My room is larger than that of my friend. This umbrella is finer than that which we have bought. Have you taken my pen or that of my sister? This is not your pencil; it is that of my brother. I speak of my book and of that of your friend. Louisa has lost her thimble and that of her mother. Thou hast eaten my apple and that of my cousin. My watch is better than that of my cousin (fem.). I have received your letter and that of your brother.

49.

Heinrich, Henry; Luise, Louisa;
Heinrich's, Henry's; Luisens, Louisa's;
dem Heinrich, to Henry; der Luise, to Louisa;
von Heinrich, of or from Henry; von Luisen, of or from Louisa.
Wilhelm, William; Wien, Vienna; Köln, Cologne;
Johann, John; Aachen, Aix-la-Chapelle;
Emilie, Emily; Lyon, Lyons;
heißt, is called; geht, goes; wohnt, lives.
Er heißt Karl, his name is Charles.

The hat of Henry, der Hut Heinrich's; to Brussels, nach Brüssel; at Brussels, zu or in Brüssel.

Mein Bruder heißt Heinrich und meine Schwester heißt Luise. Der Vater Wilhelm's ist angekommen. Die Mutter Luisens ist abgereist. Ludwig's Onkel ist sehr reich. Emiliens Hut ist sehr schön. Haben Sie diesen Hund von Heinrich oder von Ferdinand erhalten? Amalie hat dem Johann ihre Feder geliehen. Karl hat der Emilie eine Blume gegeben. Gehört dieser Garten dem Ludwig oder der Karoline? Wo ist Wilhelm? Er ist mit Karl und Joseph ausgegangen. Wohnt Ihr Onkel in Brüssel oder in Paris? Geht Ihr Vetter nach Wien oder nach Berlin? Ist Paris größer als Lyon? Ist Ihr Freund von Köln oder von Aachen?

Obs. The proper names of persons are declined with or without an article. If declined with the article, they remain unchanged. Without the article the feminine names ending in e add ns in the Genitive and n in the Dative.

50.

My cousin's name is John. The daughter of our gardener's wife is called Jane (Johanna). Art thou Charles's or Ferdinand's brother? Where are Henry and Lewis? They are in my father's room; they are gone out with William. Have you lent your pen to Henry? Who has given this flower to Louisa? We have received a letter from Lewis; he is at Dusseldorf. The sister of Charles is very short. The bonnet of Josephine is too large. My uncle lives in Vienna and my cousin in Paris. My friend goes to Cologne. William is arrived from Amsterdam. Have you seen John and Lewis? My garden is larger than that of Emily. Louisa is gone out with her mother. Henry is departed with his friend Ferdinand.

Part II.

51.

Nom. die Tische, the tables;
Gen. der Tische, of the tables;
Dat. den Tischen, to the tables;
Acc. die Tische, the tables.

Obs. Substantives of one syllable take e in the plural. Those nouns the radical vowel of which is a, o, u, au, generally change it into ä, ö, ü, äu. The Dative plural of all substantives terminates in n.

Die Freunde meines Vaters sind angekommen. Die Söhne unsers Nachbars sind sehr fleißig. Die Stühle, welche wir gekauft haben, sind sehr schön. Haben Sie die Städte Wien und Berlin gesehen? Karl hat die Hüte Wilhelm's und Ferdinand's gefunden. Mein Vater hat die Briefe Ihres Onkels nicht erhalten. Das Eisen und das Silber sind Metalle. Die Pferde sind nützlicher als die Hunde. Die Mägde eures Nachbars sind sehr fleißig. Die Aerzte in dieser Stadt sind sehr reich. Wem haben Sie die Stöcke meines Bruders gegeben? Die Thiere, welche wir in Ihrem Garten gesehen haben, sind sehr stark. Haben Sie den Freunden Heinrich's geschrieben? Gebet diesen Hund den Söhnen meines Bruders. Wir sprechen von den Briefen des Arztes.

52.

Thy brother has bought the dogs of my neighbour. The friends of Charles are ill. Have you seen the horses of our uncle? Who has written the letters of my brother? Where are the hats that you have bought? I have received this bird from the sons of the physician. I have given your umbrella to the maid-servants. (The) metals are very useful. (The) dogs are very faithful. Your brother is gone out with the sons of our neighbour (fem.). Cologne and Aix-la-Chapelle are towns. I speak of Henry's and William's friends.

53.

Der Zahn, the tooth; der Ring, the ring;
der Fuß, the foot; die Nuß, the nut;
die Hand, the hand, der Baum, the tree;
der Schuh, the shoe, warm, warm; rein, clean,
der Strumpf, the stocking; weiß, white.

Obs. The determinative words, as: dieser, jener, mein, dein, welcher, etc. take in the plural the same terminations as the article.

Meine Zähne sind sehr weiß. Ich habe die Füße sehr warm. Ihre Hände sind nicht rein. Hat der Schuhmacher meine Schuhe gebracht? Wer hat meine Strümpfe genommen? Sind das Ihre Strümpfe? Das sind nicht die meiner Schwester. Wo haben Sie diese Nüsse gekauft? Haben Sie meine Bäume schon gesehen? Von welchen Bäumen sprechen Sie? Von denjenigen, welche ich von dem Gärtner der Königin gekauft habe. Unsere Freunde sind schon abgereist. Wer hat diese Briefe geschrieben? Mein Vater hat seine Pferde und Hunde verkauft. Mein Nachbar hat einen Brief von seinen Söhnen erhalten, welche in Berlin sind. Hat Jemand meine Ringe gefunden? Niemand hat deine Ringe gesehen. Karl wird von seinen Freunden geliebt.

54.

Their, ihr; those, diejenigen or die.

Charles and Henry have lost their sticks. The shoemaker has not made your shoes. Where have you bought these tables and chairs? From whom have you received these pencils? My feet are very small. My sister has lost her thimbles. I have received these letters from my friends. These trees are higher than those. These animals are very fine. These servants are very lazy. Have you already seen our hats and our rings? Emily's stockings are whiter than those of

Louisa. Your teeth are not clean. My hands are very warm. I have found these nuts in my uncle's garden.

55.
Alle, all.

Das Kind, the child; das Dorf, the village;
das Buch, the book; das Blatt, the leaf;
das Haus, the house; das Loch, the hole;
das Volk, the people; das Huhn, the chicken;
das Glas, the glass; das Kalb, the calf;
das Band, the ribbon; der Wurm, the worm;
das Kleid, the dress; der Wald, the forest;
das Schloß, the castle; der Mann, the man, the husband.

Obs. All these monosyllabical nouns are exceptions from the general rule, and form their plural by adding er, and softening the radical vowel. Substantives ending in thum follow the same rule, as: Irrthum, Irrthümer (mistake).

Diese Häuser sind höher als jene. Jene Bänder sind schöner als diese. Deine Bücher sind nützlicher als die Luisens. Diese Mutter hat ihre Kinder verloren. Der König hat seine Schlösser verkauft. Von wem haben Sie diese Gläser erhalten? Wer hat diese Kleider gemacht? Dieser Mann ist schon sehr alt; er hat alle seine Zähne verloren. Wo sind Ihre Freunde? Alle meine Freunde sind ausgegangen. Diese Völker sind sehr glücklich; sie haben einen König, welcher sehr gut ist. Die Könige sind nicht immer glücklich. Heinrich und Wilhelm haben alle ihre Bücher verloren. Alle eure Briefe sind angekommen. Wir haben alle diese Nüsse in dem Walde unsers Onkels gefunden. Der Vater ist mit allen seinen Kindern abgereist. Diese Dörfer sind sehr schön. Von welchen Dörfern sprechen Sie? Welche Städte haben Sie gesehen? Sind alle diese Strümpfe für Luisen oder für Emilien? Haben Sie den Kindern des Nachbars einen Vogel gegeben? Wer hat alle diese Löcher in meinem Tische gemacht?

56.
Not yet, noch nicht.

Where are your children? My children are gone out. Their friends are arrived. Have you not yet written your letters? Who has bought all these riboons? Henrietta has lost all these books. We have seen all these houses. Have you also seen the castles of the king? Who has taken all my nuts? These children have lost their hats. Give these glasses to Henry and these rings to Louisa. This tree has lost all its leaves. My neighbour has sold all his chickens.

57.

der Stiefel, the boot;	der Kutscher, the coachman;
der Spiegel, the mirror;	das Fenster, the window;
der Löffel, the spoon;	das Mädchen, the girl;
die Nadel, the needle;	der Engländer, the Englishman;
die Gabel, the fork;	der Italiener, the Italian.

Obs. Masc. and neuter substantives ending in er, el, en, do not change in the plural; the feminine nouns ending in er and el take n, except: die Mütter, the mothers; die Töchter, the daughters; der Vetter, the cousin, die Vettern.

Die Schneider und Schuhmacher in dieser Stadt sind alle reich. Diese Engländer sind sehr fleißig. Meine Brüder sind alle krank. Haben Sie meine Schwestern gesehen? Wo haben Sie diese Messer, Löffel und Gabeln gekauft? Die Fenster Ihres Zimmers sind offen. Karl und Heinrich sind meine Vettern. Wir haben diese Vögel in dem Walde gefunden. Die Tiger sind sehr stark. Diese Mädchen sind sehr glücklich. Sind meine Töchter ausgegangen? Sind meine Zimmer nicht sehr schön? Hat ihre Tante alle diese Spiegel gekauft? Wer hat die Bücher und Federn dieses Mädchens genommen? Wem gehören diese Gärten und Häuser? Luise und Henriette haben ihre Nadeln verloren. Der Schuhmacher hat Ihre Schuhe und Stiefel noch nicht gebracht. Wer sind jene Männer? Es sind Italiener; es sind die Onkel meines Freundes. Diese Mütter sind sehr traurig; sie haben alle ihre Kinder verloren.

58.

The shoemaker has brought your shoes and boots. The houses of this village are all very fine. Bring us (bringen Sie uns) the spoons, forks, and knives. Where have you bought these needles? Your brothers and sisters are not come. Lewis and Ferdinand are cousins. Our mothers have seen the gardens of the king. My sons have bought the mirrors of my neighbour. (The) horses are bigger than (the) tigers. Are my stockings clean? Are your shoes new?

59.

Eins (ein), one;	vier, four;
zwei, two;	fünf, five;
drei, three;	sechs, six;

sieben, seven;	neunzehn, nineteen;
acht, eight;	zwanzig, twenty;
neun, nine;	die Aufgabe, the task, exercise;
zehn, ten;	das Jahr, the year;
elf, eleven;	die Woche, the week;
zwölf, twelve;	der Monat, the month (pl. e);
dreizehn, thirteen;	der Tag, the day;
vierzehn, fourteen;	die Stunde, the hour;
funfzehn, fifteen;	der Knabe, the boy;
sechszehn, sixteen;	seit, since (Dat.);
siebenzehn, seventeen;	es gibt, es ist, there is;
achtzehn, eighteen;	es gibt, es sind, there are;
gemacht, made, done.	

Obs. Substantives ending in e take n in the plural.

In unserm Hause sind vierzehn Zimmer. In diesem Zimmer sind zwei Tische und zwölf Stühle. Unser Nachbar hat fünf Kinder: drei Söhne und zwei Töchter. Wir haben vier Katzen und drei Hunde. In eurem Garten sind funfzehn Bäume. Das Jahr hat zwölf Monate; der Monat hat vier Wochen; die Woche hat sieben Tage. Ich habe von meinem Vater sechs Aepfel und acht Birnen erhalten. Mein Onkel hat meiner Schwester ein Federmesser und zwanzig Federn gegeben. Hast du schon alle deine Aufgaben gemacht? Johann hat noch nicht seine Aufgabe gemacht. Mein Bruder ist schon drei Jahre in Berlin. Haben Sie noch nicht gegessen? Ich habe schon seit drei Stunden gegessen. Ist Ihr Vater noch nicht angekommen? Er ist schon seit zwei Tagen angekommen. Mein Onkel ist seit vier Monaten krank; er hat seit acht Tagen nichts gegessen. Mein Bruder ist neun Jahre alt, aber meine Schwester ist noch nicht sieben Jahre alt.

60.

My father has three houses and two gardens. This man has five boys and four girls. My friend has seven sisters. We have received six letters. In this town there are twenty physicians. My cousins (fem.) have bought two cats. My cousin is seventeen years and two months old. My mother has bought six knives, twelve forks, and eighteen spoons. Our joiner has made three tables and ten chairs. We have received this week fifteen chickens and three calves. William has eaten five apples, four pears, and eleven nuts. Henry is arrived three days ago (since three days). My uncle is departed a twelvemonth ago (since a year). Charles and Ferdinand have made six exercises. There are two holes in this door. The gardener has given three flowers to my children.

61.

Das Brot, the bread; Brot, some or any bread;
das Fleisch, the meat; Fleisch, some meat;
die Aepfel, the apples; Aepfel, some apples.

Der Wein, the wine;
das Bier, the beer;
das Wasser, the water;
das Gemüse, the vegetables;
der Zucker, the sugar;
der Kaffee, the coffee;
geben Sie mir, give me;

die Kirsche, the cherry;
die Pflaume, the plum;
die Tinte, the ink;
die Suppe, the soup;
man findet, one finds, they find;
getrunken, drunk;
bringen Sie uns, bring us.

Ich habe Brot und Fleisch gegessen. Wir haben Kirschen und Pflaumen gekauft. Mein Bruder hat Wein getrunken und ihr habt Bier und Wasser getrunken. Der Schuhmacher macht Schuhe und Stiefel. Der Tischler macht Tische und Stühle. Bei diesem Kaufmann findet man Bücher, Federn, Tinte und Bleistifte. Geben Sie mir Suppe und Gemüse. Hier ist Wein und Wasser, und da ist Kaffee und Milch. Haben Sie auch Zucker? Wir haben Messer und Gabeln, Tassen und Gläser gekauft. Der Gärtner hat der Luise Kirschen und Blumen gegeben. Haben Sie schon Kaffee getrunken? In jenem Hause findet man Spiegel, Regenschirme, Bänder, Fingerhüte und Nadeln. Meine Freundin hat von ihrem Onkel Birnen und Nüsse erhalten. Wir haben Löwen, Tiger, Katzen und Hunde gesehen. In dieser Stadt gibt es Schneider und Schuhmacher, welche sehr reich sind.

62.

Wollen Sie? will you (have)? gefälligst, if you please.

Will you have some wine or some beer, some milk or some water? Give me, if you please, some soup, vegetables, meat, and bread. Where does one find (finds one) ink and pens? Are you a father? Have you children? Has your father bought any trees or flowers? My brother has books and friends. Here is coffee and sugar. My neighbour has birds, dogs, and horses. We are speaking of towns and villages, of houses and gardens. Iron and silver are metals. Vienna and Berlin are towns. What have you done? We have done exercises (Aufgaben gemacht), we have written letters. We have eaten apples and plums, and we have drunk some wine and beer.

63.

Wenig, little, few;	zu, too; wie? how?
viel, much;	das Obst, die Frucht, the fruit;
viele, many;	das Geld, the money;
genug, enough;	der Pfeffer, the pepper;
mehr, more;	das Salz, the salt;
weniger, less, fewer;	der Senf, the mustard.

Heinrich hat viel Geld; er hat mehr Geld als ich. Geben Sie mir ein wenig Fleisch. Ich habe genug Brot. Du hast zu viel Salz und Pfeffer. Wir haben weniger Obst als ihr. Luise hat weniger Federn als Henriette. Karl hat mehr Aufgaben gemacht als Ludwig. Hast du so viel Geld als mein Bruder? Der Arme hat wenig Freunde. Es gibt wenig Menschen, welche zufrieden sind. Geben Sie der Henriette nicht zu viel Senf. Mein Bruder hat zu viel Wein getrunken. Diese Mutter hat viele Kinder. Dieser Mann hat viele Blumen. Wie viele Hunde hat Ihr Vater? Es gibt dieses Jahr wenig Kirschen, aber viele Pflaumen. Mein Freund hat diese Woche mehr Briefe erhalten als ich. Hat dein Vater so viele Bücher als mein Onkel? Geben Sie mir gefälligst ein wenig Tinte. Wollen Sie noch mehr? Ich habe genug.

64.

There is much fruit this year. Our gardener has many trees and flowers. Will you have a little meat or some vegetables? Have you mustard enough? I have salt and pepper enough. Our neighbour has much money; he is very rich. Give a little wine to this woman. This man has few friends, but he has many dogs and cats. There are many birds in this forest. How many physicians are there in your town? Have you as many apples and pears as we? We have not so many as you, but we have more plums and nuts than you. Charles has fewer friends than Henry. This tree has fewer leaves than that one. There are too many chairs in this room.

65.

Das Stück, the piece;	das Dutzend, the dozen;
die Flasche, the bottle;	der Korb, the basket;
die Tasse, the cup;	die Leinwand, the linen;
das Pfund, the pound;	das Taschentuch, the pocket-handkerchief;
die Elle, the yard, ell;	
das Paar, the pair;	der Handschuh, the glove;

das Hemd, the shirt;   der Käse, the cheese;
die Halsbinde, the cravat;   der Schinken, the ham.

Obs. The words Pfund, Paar and Dutzend, are invariable when they are preceded by a number. — The English word *of* which follows the names of weights and measures is not expressed in German.

Meine Mutter hat der Henriette drei Paar Handschuhe, sechs Paar Strümpfe, zwei Dutzend Hemden und einen Korb Kirschen geschickt. In diesem Koffer sind zehn Ellen Leinwand, vier Taschentücher und sechs Halsbinden. Mein Bruder hat zwei Paar Schuhe und ein Paar Stiefel gekauft. Wir haben dem Freunde unsers Onkels zwanzig Pfund Zucker und zehn Flaschen Wein geschickt. Geben Sie mir ein Stück Käse, eine Flasche Bier und ein wenig Senf. Ich habe ein Glas Wein getrunken und ein Stück Schinken gegessen. Wir haben bei unserer Freundin eine Tasse Kaffee getrunken. Geben Sie mir ein Glas Wasser und ein Stück Zucker. Meine Schwester hat zwei Pfund Kirschen und ein Pfund Pflaumen gekauft. Wir haben ein Dutzend Stühle bei dem Tischler unsers Onkels gekauft. Ich habe von dem Gärtner einen Korb Blumen erhalten.

66.

The shoemaker has made a pair of shoes for Louisa and two pair of boots for William. We have drunk two glasses of wine and three glasses of beer. Give me a bottle of water and a little meat and bread. Will you have a piece of ham or cheese? My aunt has bought a dozen of cravats, two dozen of shirts and, ten pair of gloves and stockings. How many shirts have you? I have three dozen. This linen is very fine; how many yards have you bought? I have bought twenty yards. That is not enough for ten shirts. My uncle has given to Henry a penknife, twenty pens, two cravats, and a pair of gloves. Ferdinand has bought a pound of plums, six pounds of coffee, and two yards of ribbon. Will you have a cup of coffee or a glass of wine? Give me, if you please, a glass of water.

67.

Sing. guter, gute, gutes;   *Plur.* gute.

schlecht, bad;   vortrefflich, excellent;
kalt, cold;   liebenswürdig, amiable;
hübsch, pretty;   das Papier, the paper;
todt, dead;   das Geschäft, the affair, business.

Obs. If the adjective is not preceded by an article or any other determinative word, it takes the terminations of dieser, diese, dieses.

Hier ist guter Schinken, gute Suppe und gutes Brod. Haben Sie gutes Papier und gute Tinte? Wir haben schlechten Wein und gutes Bier getrunken. Unser Gärtner hat vortreffliches Obst. Unsere Magd hat guten Senf, aber schlechten Pfeffer gekauft. Eduard hat gute Freunde und nützliche Bücher. Mein Onkel hat schöne Gärten und große Häuser. Euer Nachbar hat treue Hunde. Johann, geben Sie mir ein Glas Wasser! Wollen Sie kaltes oder warmes Wasser? Meine Schwester hat ein Paar hübsche Handschuhe gekauft. Euer Bruder spricht immer von gutem Wein und guter Suppe, aber nicht von nützlichen Büchern, von Aufgaben und Geschäften. Paris und London sind schöne Städte. Heinrich hat ein Paar neue Schuhe erhalten.

68.

Have you any good mustard? We have good bread and good meat. Your gardener has very fine flowers. These children have fine dresses. We have faithful friends, amiable brothers, and useful books. Give me some better cheese and better beer. At (bei) this merchant's one finds pretty gloves, fine penknives, and good pens. Iron and silver are very useful metals. You have always excellent wine. My brother is not gone out, he has too many affairs. Henry has bought good paper and good ink. We speak of good coffee, of excellent fruit, and new dresses.

69.

Ein guter, eine gute, ein gutes.

Golden, of gold, golden; gesund, healthy, wholesome;
silbern, of silver; kein, no, none.

Obs. If the adjective is preceded by the indefinite article, by kein or by a possessive pronoun, as: mein, dein, unser etc., it takes in the Nominative Sing. the terminations er, e, es, and in all other cases en, except the Accusative fem. and neuter, which is the same as the Nominative.

Unser Gärtner ist ein guter Mann. Eure Gärtnerin ist eine gute Frau. Emilie ist ein gutes Kind. Wir haben einen guten Vater und eine gute Mutter. Heinrich hat ein schönes Pferd und einen schönen Hund. Luise hat große Zähne, aber eine kleine Hand und einen kleinen Fuß. Ferdinand ist mit meinem jüngern Bruder ausgegangen. Henriette ist mit meiner ältern Schwester abgereist. Geben Sie dieses Brot einem armen Kinde. Dieses Federmesser gehört einem jungen Manne, der bei unserm Nachbar wohnt. Ludwig ist der Sohn eines reichen Kaufmanns. Haben Sie guten Wein oder gutes Bier? Wir haben keinen guten Wein und kein gutes Bier. Wer hat meine silberne Uhr und meinen goldenen Ring genommen? Wir haben unsern besten Freund verloren. Eure kleinen Kinder sind sehr gesund. Es gibt keine guten Kirschen dieses Jahr. Mein Onkel hat seine schönsten Pferde verkauft. Bist du mit deinen neuen Stiefeln zufrieden? Hast du schon von unsern guten Pflaumen gegessen?

70.

Charles is a good boy. Henrietta is a pretty girl. That is a happy mother. That is an excellent wine. Where is my little Henry, my good Louisa? We have a very rich uncle. William has an old father. Iron is a useful metal. The dog is a faithful animal. I have received a new umbrella and a golden watch. My neighbour has done much business this year. Give this bottle of wine to a poor man or to a poor woman. I have no friend in this town. Have you no good pens for this child? Our best friends are dead. This joiner makes no good chairs.

71.

Der gute, die gute, das gute.

Gestern, yesterday;   der Schüler, the pupil, schoolboy;
heute, to-day;   die Schule, the school;
ich liebe, I love, I like; das Leben, the life.

Obs. When the adjective is preceded by the definite article, or any other determinative word, which has the same termination, as: dieser, jener etc., it takes in the Nominative Sing. the final e, and in all other cases en, except the Accusative Sing. fem. and neuter.

Der gute Heinrich ist krank. Die kleine Sophie ist sehr liebenswürdig. Das arme Kind hat seine Mutter verloren. Das ist der höchste Baum in unserm Garten. Lisette ist die fleißigste von unsern Mägden. Dieser reiche Engländer wohnt bei meinem Onkel. Wo haben Sie diese goldene Nadel gefunden? Wem gehört dieses große Haus und jener schöne Garten? Franz ist mit dem kleinen Karl ausgegangen. Wir haben gestern bei der guten Emilie Kirschen gegessen. Wer wohnt in diesem schönen Schlosse? Wie heißt diese hübsche Blume? Wo haben Sie diesen schlechten Wein und dieses schlechte Bier gekauft? Ich liebe die fleißigen Schüler und die treuen Freunde. Der Löwe und der Tiger sind die stärksten Thiere. Das sind die glücklichsten Tage meines Lebens. Geben Sie diesem armen Manne ein wenig Wein. Leihen Sie diesem kleinen Mädchen Ihren Regenschirm.

72.
Every one, Jedermann.

The diligent pupil is loved by every one. The idle child is loved by nobody. The good king is loved by his people. This poor woman has no bread for her children. This rich merchant has given much money to the poor. I like the pretty flowers and the pretty children. I do not like the fine dresses. This fruit is not wholesome. My brother has found this gold ring to-day. Lewis is gone out with his little brother. The father of this young man is a shoemaker. The daughter of this old woman is ill. Have you drunk of this excellent wine? Will you (have) some of these fine plums? Which hat have you taken? I have taken the white hat. Which watch have you sold? I have sold the silver watch.

73.

der erste, the first;	unartig, naughty;
der zweite, the second;	bescheiden, modest;
der dritte, the third;	der Theil, the part;
der vierte, the fourth;	der Band, the volume;
der letzte, the last;	nur, only; die Klasse, the class.

Der wievielste? what day of the month?

Obs. Of before the name of a month is not expressed in German.

Dieser junge Mann ist sehr fleißig; er ist der erste in der Klasse. Karl ist der zweite; der bescheidene Heinrich ist der dritte; Johann ist der vierte; der kleine Wilhelm ist der fünfte; Paul ist der sechste; Franz ist der achte; Gustav ist der neunte; der unartige Eduard ist der elfte und der faule Ludwig ist der letzte. Zwei ist der fünfte Theil von zehn. Fünf ist der vierte Theil von zwanzig. Ein Tag ist der siebente Theil einer Woche. Den wievielsten des Monats haben wir heute? Wir haben heute den dreizehnten oder den vierzehnten. Ist es nicht der zwanzigste? Mein Vater ist den dritten Mai abgereist. Mein Onkel ist den zehnten December angekommen. Haben Sie den erſten und zweiten Band? Ich habe nur den erſten.

74.

Louisa is the first in the class; Maria is the second; the good Josephina is the third; Henrietta is the fifth; the modest Sophia is the ninth; Matilda (Mathilde) is the fifteenth; the naughty Caroline is the last. Three is the sixth part of eighteen. A week is the fourth part of a month; and a month is the twelfth part of a year. What day of the month is it (have we)? It is to-day the eleventh or the twelfth. We departed on the second of May and arrived on the sixteenth. Which volume have you taken? Have you taken the third and the fourth? I have only taken the third.

75.

Singular.	*Plural.*
Der meinige, die meinige, das meinige, mine;	die meinigen;
der deinige, thine;	der unſerige, ours;
der ſeinige, his;	der eurige, Ihrige, yours;
der ihrige, hers;	der ihrige, theirs;

leicht, easy, light.

Obs. Instead of: der meinige, der deinige, etc. may be said meiner, meine, meines or meins, with the terminations of dieſer, dieſe, dieſes. — The declension of der meinige, derjenige, etc. is the same as that of the adjective, preceded by the definite article.

Dein Vater iſt größer als der meinige. Meine Mutter iſt kleiner als die deinige. Unſer Buch iſt nützlicher als das Ihrige. Mein Sohn iſt nicht ſo alt als der deinige. Euer Pferd iſt jünger als das unſerige. Unſere Bücher ſind nützlicher als die eurigen. Mein Vater hat ſeine Uhr verloren; Heinrich hat auch die ſeinige verloren. Meine Schweſter hat die ihrige verkauft. Mein Vater hat deinen Brief und den meinigen geleſen. Meine Tante hat ihren Garten und den unſerigen verkauft. Hat dein Bruder meinen Stock oder den ſeinigen genommen? Hat Luiſe meinen Fingerhut oder den ihrigen gefunden? Deine Aufgaben ſind leichter als die meinigen. Dieſe Bäume ſind höher als die unſerigen. In unſerer Stadt ſind mehr Aerzte als in der eurigen.

76.

My thimble is as fine as yours. Your umbrella is not so large as mine. My son is more diligent than thine. My friend has sold his house and mine. My sister has eaten her apple and thine. Has Louisa taken my pen or hers; my pencil or hers? Henry has read my books and yours. Your sisters are younger than ours. We speak of our friend and of yours. Is my room smaller than thine? I have promised a book to your son and to mine, to your daughter and to mine. I speak of my tasks and of thine. This castle belongs to my uncle and to yours.

77.

	Singular.	Plural.
Nom.	er, he; fie, she; es, it;	fie, they;
Acc.	ihn, him; fie, her; es, it;	fie, them;

Gehabt, had; gekannt, known; ja, yes;
gelesen, read; gebracht, brought; nein, no.

Haben Sie meinen Stock? Ja, ich habe ihn. Haben Sie meine Uhr? Nein, ich habe Sie nicht. Haben fie mein Messer? Ich habe es nicht. Haben Sie meine Schuhe? Ja, ich habe fie. Wo ist mein Hund? Ich habe ihn nicht gesehen. Wer hat meine Feder genommen? Dein Bruder hat fie genommen. Wo hast du dieses Taschentuch gefunden? Ich habe es in Ihrem Zimmer gefunden. Diese Vögel sind sehr schön. Von wem hast du fie erhalten? Deine Schwester ist sehr fleißig; meine Mutter liebt fie sehr. Haben Sie meinen Oheim gekannt? Ich habe ihn nicht gekannt. Dies ist ein nützliches Buch; haben Sie es schon gelesen? Wo ist mein Fingerhut? Ich habe ihn Ihrer Schwester gegeben; fie hat ihn verloren. Hat Jemand meine Gabel genommen? Karl hat fie genommen. Wem hat der Gärtner alle diese Blumen geschickt? Er hat fie Ihrer Mutter geschickt. Hat Heinrich deinen Bleistift gehabt? Nein, er hat ihn heute nicht gehabt.

78.

Has the shoemaker brought my boot? Yes, he has brought it. Hast thou already done thy task? I have not yet done it. Have you seen my new room? No, I have not yet seen it. Where hast thou bought these pretty rings? I have bought them in Paris. Who has had my penknife? I have not had it, your brother has had it. I have received a letter from my aunt, have you read it? Have you already seen the king? I have not yet seen him. You have a good pen; lend it to my sister. There is your brother; do you see him? Do you not see him? Where are your gloves? Lend them to your aunt. Where is your umbrella? Give it to this child. My aunt is dead; did you know her? Which books have you there? Have you read them? Where is thy dog? My father has sold it.

79.

Ich bin gewesen, I have been;
du bist gewesen, thou hast been;
er ist gewesen, he has been;
wir sind gewesen, we have been;
ihr seid gewesen, you have been;
sie sind gewesen, they have been.

Herr, Mr.;
der Herr, the gentleman;
Fräulein, Miss;
das Fräulein, the young lady;
Madame, Madam, Mrs.;
die Dame, the lady;
zusammen, together;
lange, long, a long time;
der Morgen, the morning;
das Viertel, the quarter;
ein halber, e, es, half a.

Das erste mal, the first time; das letzte mal, the last time; ein mal, once; zwei mal, twice.

Obs. The word Herr takes in all cases of the Singular n, and in all cases of the Plural en. It is also used with the article in the sense of Mr. — In speaking politely, the words Herr, Frau and Fräulein are used as a title, as in French, for instance: Ihr Herr Vater, your father; Ihre Frau Mutter, your mother; Ihre Fräulein Schwestern, your sisters.

Wer ist hier gewesen? Herr Moll ist hier gewesen; er hat dieses Buch gebracht. Bist du bei dem Schuhmacher gewesen? Ich bin heute bei deinem Schuhmacher gewesen; er hat Ihre Stiefel schon gemacht. Wo seid ihr diesen Morgen gewesen? Wir sind bei unserm Freunde Karl gewesen, welcher sehr krank ist. Dieser Herr ist drei Jahre in Wien gewesen, und seine Brüder sind sehr lange in Konstantinopel gewesen. Du bist nicht fleißig gewesen, du hast deine Aufgaben noch nicht gemacht. Ich bin gestern bei Madame Röber gewesen; sie ist eine sehr liebenswürdige Frau. Ist Fräulein N. oft in dieser Stadt gewesen? Sie ist schon drei mal hier gewesen. Haben Sie den Herrn Scholl gekannt? Ich habe ihn in Berlin gekannt; wir sind oft zusammen ausgegangen. Wie lange sind Sie in Madrid gewesen? Ich bin nur ein halbes Jahr da gewesen, aber ich bin drei Viertel Jahr in Lissabon gewesen. Haben Sie die Herren Nolleb schon gesehen? Ich habe sie gestern bei einem meiner Freunde gesehen.

80.

Have they (has one) brought my shoes? Yes, they have brought them. Has the tailor been here? No, he has not yet been here. Hast thou been at the joiner's? No, I have not yet been there. We have many flowers; we have been in the garden of (the) Mr. Nollet. Have you also been at Mr. Moll's? My brother has never been more contented than to-day; he has received from his uncle a beautiful gold watch, and half a dozen pocket-handkerchiefs. How long have you been in Paris? We have been there six months. These gentlemen have done much business; they have been very happy. Are Messrs. N. already departed to Cologne? They are departed this morning with their uncle; I have seen them at Mrs. Sicard's.

81.

Ich war, I was;
du warst, thou wast;
er war, he was;
wir waren, we were;
ihr waret, you were;
sie waren, they were.

Ehemals, formerly; warum, why? als, when.

Obs. When a sentence begins with als, when, the verb is placed at the end of the phrase.

Wo warst du diesen Morgen? Ich war bei meinem Vetter, welcher von Frankfurt angekommen ist. Mein Bruder und ich, wir waren bei deinem Vater. Ihre Tante war schon abgereist. Herr Moll war ehemals sehr reich; er hat seit zehn Jahren viel verloren. Waren Sie noch nicht bei Herrn Mably? Ich bin gestern dagewesen, aber er war ausgegangen. Wie alt war Ihr Bruder, als er in Köln war? Er war zehn oder elf Jahre alt. Wir waren nicht zusammen; er war in Köln und ich war in Düsseldorf. Meine Schwestern waren lange in Brüssel bei Herrn Nollet. Warum sind Sie gestern nicht gekommen? Ich war gestern krank. Waren diese Herren immer so reich? Haben Sie immer so viele Freunde gehabt? Warst du diesen Morgen in der Schule? Ich bin heute nicht in der Schule gewesen.

82.

I was formerly much happier; I was young and strong. Wast thou always as contented as to-day? My father was formerly very rich. You were gone out when I came (I am come). Where were you when we (are) arrived? My sisters were very ill yesterday. How old were you when you were at N.? I was fifteen years and six months old. Was my room open when you came (you are come)? No, but the windows were open. This girl was much prettier when she was young. John and William were always my brother's friends. Were you not with my brother when he (has) lost his handkerchief?

83.

Ich hatte, I had;
du hattest, thou hadst;
er hatte, he had;
wir hatten, we had;
ihr hattet, you had;
sie hatten, they had.

Die Aeltern, the parents;   der Besuch, the visit;
der Handel, the commerce;   der andere, the other.

Wir hatten diese Woche den Besuch der Herren Moll, welche mit ihrer Schwester angekommen sind. Ihr hattet viele Freunde, als ihr noch jung waret. Wir hatten mehr Bücher als ihr. Unser Onkel hatte ehemals viele Pferde und Hunde. Du warst sehr fleißig, als du noch deine Aeltern hattest. Diese zwei Kaufleute waren ehemals sehr reich; sie hatten einen großen Handel. Ich hatte zwei Brüder; der eine war in Wien, der andere in Berlin. Hast du meine zwei Brüder gekannt? Ich habe denjenigen gekannt, welcher in Berlin war; der andere war jünger als ich. Wo ist euer Vetter, der so viele Vögel hatte? Er ist seit einem Jahre in Brüssel. Mein Federmesser war verloren; Ihr Bruder hat es gefunden. Hattet ihr eure Briefe schon geschrieben, als wir ausgegangen sind? Wir hatten sie noch nicht geschrieben; wir hatten keine guten Federn und kein gutes Papier.

84.

Der Verstand, the intellect; die Güte, the kindness.

Mr. Maury was formerly much happier; he had many friends, much money, many horses and dogs. Henry is dead; he was a good boy, he had so much intellect and kindness, he was loved by every body. We were often in his garden; his sisters were very amiable and they had many flowers and books. His parents were not rich, but they had a great trade. was ill yesterday; I had eaten too much fruit. Hadst thou not yet done thy exercises when I came (I am come)? No, I had not yet done them. My brother had already done his when thou camest (art come).

85.

Mir, to me, me;	ihm, to him, him;
Dir, to thee, thee;	ihr, to her, her.

zu, to.

kaufen, to buy;	schreiben, to write;
verkaufen, to sell;	lesen, to read;
geben, to give;	sehen, to see;
leihen, to lend;	(die) Lust, a mind;
thun, to do;	die Zeit, the time;
machen, to make, to do;	das Vergnügen, the pleasure.

Ich kann, I can; du kannst, thou canst; er kann, he can; wir können we can; ihr könnet, you can; sie können, they can.

Obs. The Infinitive is placed at the end of the sentence.

Kannst du mir dieses Buch leihen? Ich kann dir dieses Buch nicht leihen; es gehört meinem Vetter Heinrich. Wer kann diesen Brief lesen? Ich kann ihn lesen; er ist sehr gut geschrieben. Wir können diesen Morgen nicht schreiben. Warum könnet ihr nicht schreiben? Wir haben keine Tinte. Können Sie meinem Bruder Ihre Uhr leihen? Ich kann ihm meine Uhr nicht leihen, ich habe sie dem Herrn S. verkauft. Haben Sie meiner Schwester eine Feder gegeben? Ich habe ihr keine Feder gegeben. Haben Sie Lust, diesen Hund zu kaufen? Ich habe keine Lust, ihn zu kaufen; er ist nicht treu. Hat Ihr Bruder heute nichts zu thun? Er hat drei Briefe zu schreiben. Wir haben noch zwei Aufgaben zu machen. Ich habe gestern das Vergnügen gehabt, Ihre Fräulein Schwester zu sehen. Haben Sie Zeit, diesen Brief zu lesen? Ich habe jetzt nicht Zeit, ihn zu lesen. Können Sie mir einen Regenschirm geben? Ich kann Ihnen keinen geben, ich habe nur einen. Ihr Herr Bruder hat die Güte, mir den seinigen zu leihen. Sind Sie gestern bei meiner Tante gewesen? Nein, ich war gestern nicht bei ihr; ich hatte zu viele Geschäfte.

86.

Can you do that? Yes, I can (it); but my brother cannot. Will you lend me your penknife? I cannot lend thee my penknife; my sister has taken it. Have you given a pen to my cousin? Yes, I have given him one. Hast thou sold thy dog to my sister? I have not sold her my dog. Canst thou not do thy exercise? I cannot do it to-day. We can read this book. These gentlemen cannot write their letters; they have no paper. Hast thou a mind to buy a pair of boots? Has your brother a mind to sell his ring? Have you had the kindness to give a glass of water to this poor man? My friend has had the pleasure to see his parents. I have not had time to read all these letters. My father has had the kindness to buy me a golden watch. Hast thou seen it? I have not yet seen it. Have you been with Ferdinand to-day? I have been with him this morning.

87.

Uns, to us, us; euch, Ihnen, to you, you; ihnen, to them, them;
Gehen, to go; haben, to have;
kommen, to come; sein, to be; wenn, if;
trinken, to drink; unwohl; indisposed;
essen, to eat; jetzt, now, at present.

Ich will, I will; du willst, thou wilt; er will, he will; wir wollen, we will; ihr wollet, you will; sie wollen, they will.

Willst du mit mir gehen? Ich kann nicht mit dir gehen, ich habe keine Zeit. Ich will dir ein schönes Buch leihen, wenn du fleißig bist. Kann dein Bruder heute nicht kommen? Er hat keine Lust zu kommen; er ist unwohl. Wir wollen jetzt unsere Aufgaben machen. Wollen Sie ein Glas Wein trinken? Ich habe schon ein Glas Bier getrunken. Ich will ein Stück Fleisch oder Käse essen. Wollen Sie ein wenig Senf und Salz? Können Sie uns diesen Stock leihen? Ich kann Ihnen diesen Stock nicht leihen, mein Bruder will ihn haben. Man kann nicht unglücklicher sein, als dieser junge Mann; er hat seine Aeltern und seine Brüder und Schwestern verloren. Wer will diesen Apfel haben? Ich will ihn haben. Was willst du jetzt thun? Ich will ein paar Briefe schreiben. Ich will euch einen Korb Kirschen geben, wenn ihr fleißig sein wollet. Wollen Sie die Güte haben, mir eine Nadel zu geben? Ich habe jetzt keine, ich kann Ihnen keine geben. Haben Sie Zeit, mit uns zu gehen? Ich habe keine Zeit, mit Ihnen zu gehen. Haben Sie den Herren N. schon einen Besuch gemacht? Ich habe ihnen diesen Morgen einen Besuch gemacht.

88.

What hast thou to do? I have nothing to do. Wilt thou read this book? Yes, I will read it. How is thy brothre? He is indisposed, he cannot come. Where can one buy these fine penknives? One can buy them at the merchant's who lives at our neighbour's. Will you give me a little ink? Can your sister lend me her penknife? What do these gentlemen want (what will, etc.)? These ladies will buy an umbrella. One cannot be more unhappy than I (am), one cannot have more misfortune than I. Give us something to drink. What will you (have)? Will you have wine or beer? I have lent you my stick. Where are your brothers? I have sold them my dog. This man is very rich; all these houses belong to him.

89.

Mich, me, myself; dich, thee, thyself;
uns, us, ourselves; euch, you, yourselves;
sich, one's self, him-, her-, itself, themselves.

Loben, to praise;	gelobt, praised;
lieben, to love, like;	geliebt, loved;
besuchen, to visit;	besucht, visited;
schlagen, to beat;	geschlagen, beaten;
sich schlagen, to fight;	der Lehrer, the master;
waschen, to wash;	gewaschen, washed.

Der Lehrer hat dich gelobt, weil du fleißig gewesen bist. Dein Bruder ist ein böser Knabe; er hat mich gestern geschlagen. Hast du dich schon gewaschen? Ich habe mich noch nicht gewaschen; aber Heinrich hat sich schon seit einer Stunde gewaschen. Warum willst du meinen Hund schlagen? Er hat mein Brot genommen. Unsere Aeltern sind unsere besten Freunde; wir wollen sie immer lieben. Karl, du bist sehr unartig; man kann dich nicht lieben. Wie viele Gläser Wein hast du getrunken? Ich habe nur eine halbe Flasche getrunken. Wo bist du diesen Morgen gewesen? Ich bin mit meinem Vater bei Herrn N. gewesen. Ist Herr N. noch immer unwohl? Er ist seit gestern ein wenig besser; aber er kann noch nicht essen und trinken. Der Arzt war heute zwei mal bei ihm. Ich will ihn morgen auch besuchen, oder ihm einen kleinen Brief schreiben. Aber warum haben Sie uns noch nicht besucht? Ich habe noch keine Zeit gehabt, Sie zu besuchen.

90.

Who has beaten thee? Your cousin has beaten me. With whom wilt thou fight? I will not fight. I have no mind to fight. Lewis will fight with Henry. The servant has not yet washed my shirts. She will wash them now. I have sold you my penknife, but you have not yet given me the money. Your children have been very good (artig) to-day; the master has praised them very (much); he has given them a beautiful book and a basket of cherries. Why has the master not yet visited us? He has no time; he is always in his school. He is an amiable man; he is loved by all his pupils. There is Ferdinand; hast thou washed thyself, my child? Yes, mamma (Mama), I have already washed myself.

91.

Sagen, to say, to tell; glauben, to believe;
schicken, to send; wissen, to know.
Müssen, must; ich muß, I must; du mußt, thou must; er muß, he must; wir müssen, we must; ihr müsset, you must; sie müssen, they must.

Obs. The Accusative of the personal pronoun is placed before the Dative.

Können Sie mir sagen, wo Herr Moll wohnt? Ich ann es Ihnen nicht sagen. Wollen Sie mir diese Feder leihen? Ich kann sie Ihnen nicht leihen, sie gehört mir nicht. Ich muß heute dem Fräulein S. einen Besuch machen, sie ist gestern mit ihrer Mutter angekommen. Mußt du jetzt schon gehen? Wo sind meine Schuhe? Hat der Schuhmacher sie noch nicht gebracht? Nein, er will sie dir in einer Stunde schicken. Wie kannst du das wissen? Er hat es mir gesagt. Ich kann es nicht glauben. Dein Bruder muß noch seine Aufgaben machen. Wir müssen Alles thun, was unsere Aeltern und Lehrer wollen. Ihr müsset meinen Vetter einmal besuchen; er ist seit drei Wochen krank. Heinrich und Wilhelm müssen viele Bücher haben. Wer hat dir diesen Ring gegeben? Meine Tante hat ihn mir gegeben. Luise, ich will dir etwas sagen; du hast meine Schere genommen. Ich habe es schon gesehen, Mutter. Wollen Sie meiner Schwester diesen Fingerhut geben? Ich will ihn ihr jetzt geben. Wer hat Ihnen diesen Brief geschrieben? Meine Base hat ihn mir geschrieben.

92.

My friend has had the kindness to send me a basket of cherries. You have not yet sent me my book. I have not yet had time to send it you. Who has taken my pen? I cannot tell (it) thee. Wilt thou not believe me? This penknife belongs to my brother; thou must give it him. Charles will not lend me his umbrella. Why will he not lend it thee? My uncle is arrived. Your brother has told (it) us. Who must do that? Your sisters must do it. You must tell it to Mr. Moll. This letter is not well written; I cannot read it. Hast thou my stick? No, I have it not. I have lent it to you. You have not lent it to me.

Part III.

93.

Ich lobe, I praise, I am praising, I do praise;
du lobest, du lobst, thou praisest, etc.;
er lobet, er lobt, he praises;
wir loben, we praise;
ihr lobet, ihr lobt, you praise;
sie loben, they praise.

Finden, to find;	das Tuch, the cloth;
wohnen, to live, to dwell;	die Straße, the street;
bringen, to bring;	suchen, to seek, to look for.
theuer, dear;	

Was suchen Sie? Ich suche meine Feder. Mein Bruder sucht seinen Bleistift. Wir suchen unsern Hund. Diese Kinder suchen ihre Bücher. Wo kaufen Sie Ihr Papier? Wir kaufen unser Papier bei dem Buchhändler. Ich finde meinen Stock nicht. Wer hat meinen Stock genommen? Ich glaube, daß Ihr Bruder ihn genommen hat. Ich liebe diesen Knaben nicht, er ist immer unartig. Du liebst deinen Lehrer. Gott liebt die guten Menschen. Gute Kinder lieben ihre Aeltern. Ist es wahr, daß Ihr Onkel sein Haus verkauft? Wie theuer verkaufen Sie die Elle von diesem Tuche? Ich verkaufe die Elle dieses Tuches zu vier Thaler. Das ist sehr theuer. Findest du nicht, Heinrich, daß das sehr theuer ist? Ja, ich finde es sehr theuer. Wir verkaufen aber viel von diesem Tuche. Jedermann findet es schön. Schicken Sie mir drei und eine halbe Elle. Wissen Sie, wo ich wohne?

Ja, Sie wohnen in der Petersstraße. Meine Magd kann es Ihnen heute noch bringen.

94.

tadeln, to blame;   Alles, all, every thing;
arbeiten, to work: Alles was all that.

What are you doing? I am reading the book which your brother has lent me. You read too much. Why do you not write? I have already written three letters. My cousins never write. You always blame your cousins; one must blame nobody. What art thou doing? I am doing my exercise. What is thy sister doing? She is working. What do you drink? I drink wine and my brother drinks beer. We drink no wine. I eat cherries. My brothers eat plums. You are always eating, but you do not work. Can you tell me where Mr. N. lives? He lives in (the) William street. Livest thou with thy uncle? No, I do not live with him. Dost thou go to Paris? No, I do not go to Paris. I do not like this young man; he always blames his friends. He will never lend me his penknife. I lend him all that I have. We lend every thing to our friends. You always beat my brother; you are very naughty. These boys beat every body. Do you sell paper? I sell paper, pens, and ink. What do you say? I say that you have taken my knife.

95.

Ich lobte, I praised, did praise, was praising;
du lobtest, thou praisedst, etc.;
er lobte, he praised;
wir lobten, we praised;
ihr lobtet, you praised:
sie lobten, they praised.

Spielen, to play;   die Geschichte, the story,
lachen, to laugh;   der Abend, the evening;
tanzen, to dance;   so sehr, so much;
erzählen, to tell, relate;   ganz quite, whole;
theilen, to share, divide;   bis, till, until;
erlauben, to allow, permit;   daß, that.

Obs. The adverb so, which connects two sentences, is not translated in English.

Dein Bruder und ich, wir wohnten zu N. in dem nämlichen Hause. Wir waren den ganzen Tag zusammen. Wir machten unsere Aufgaben zusammen, wir spielten zusammen und hatten kein größeres Vergnügen, als wenn wir zusammen waren. Er liebte mich und ich liebte ihn so sehr, daß wir wie Brüder waren. Wenn dein Vater ihm etwas schickte, so theilten wir es. Ich arbeitete oft für ihn und er arbeitete für mich. Der Lehrer lobte und liebte uns. Alle gute Schüler waren unsere Freunde; sie besuchten uns jeden Tag; wir erzählten uns schöne Geschichten und lachten und tanzten, bis es Abend war. Du schicktest uns oft hübsche Bücher, welche uns viel Vergnügen machten. Wir hatten sehr oft Zeit zu lesen. Wenn wir unsere Aufgaben gemacht hatten, erlaubte der Lehrer uns immer zu spielen oder ein nützliches Buch zu lesen.

96.

Wählen, to choose; das Spiel, the play, the game;
weinen, to cry, to weep; während, while, during.

Obs. The Nominative is always placed after its verb, in a sentence, which serves to complete the preceding one: wenn er kommt, gehe ich mit ihm.

When we were young we lived in this house. Your sister bought some ribbons and chose the finest for you. Formerly I loved play, but at present I love books. This people always loved their king. Thy cousin was still looking for his hat when we (are) departed. The merchant whom thou soughtest yesterday has been here. Thy brother sold his penknife this morning. While we were crying, you were laughing and dancing. My father allowed me always to read good books and to play with my friends. We often worked together when you were living with your uncle. I danced better than you, but you did your exercises better than I. Thou wast often idle, and thou hadst not always a mind to read and to write. I told thee pretty stories, but thou lovedst play too much; thou didst play the whole day. The master blamed thee often, and the good scholars did not love thee.

97.

Ich werde loben, I shall or will praise;
du wirst loben, thou wilt praise;
er wird loben, he will praise;
wir werden loben, we shall praise;
ihr werdet loben, you will praise;
sie werden loben, they will praise.

Obs. Werden, taken in an absolute sense, signifies *to become;* but when constructed with another verb, it answers to the English auxiliary verb *shall* or *will*

Ich werde diesen Abend das Vergnügen haben, meinen Onkel zu sehen. Ich werde dir diesen hübschen Ring geben, wenn du fleißig sein wirst. Heinrich wird mir heute ein Paar schöne Handschuhe kaufen. Deine Schwester wird zufrieden sein, wenn sie ihre Aufgabe gemacht hat. Wenn wir in N. sein werden, werden wir viel Vergnügen haben. Wann werden Sie mich besuchen? Ich glaube, wir werden Sie morgen besuchen. Meine Brüder werden auch heute oder morgen kommen. Es wird meinem Vater sehr viel Vergnügen machen, sie noch einmal zu sehen. Wann werden Sie Ihrem Freunde Karl schreiben? Ich schreibe ihm in acht bis vierzehn Tagen. Wollen Sie die Güte haben, mir das Buch zu schicken, welches Sie mir versprochen haben? Ich werde es Ihnen heute schicken, Fräulein. Mein Bedienter wird es Ihnen bringen. Ich hatte es einem Freunde geliehen, der es bisjetzt gehabt hat.

98.

Müde, tired, fatigued; das Wetter, the weather; hierher, hither.

Shall you go with us? I do not believe that my father will allow me (allows it to me). Has the shoemaker brought my boots? No, he will bring them to you this evening. What shall we do now? We will drink a glass of wine. Will you have the kindness to lend me your horse? I shall lend it you with much pleasure. We shall play to-day in the garden of our uncle; he will allow (it) us. I shall tell you a beautiful story if you are good and diligent. Wilt thou work to-day? I believe that I shall not work to-day. Come hither, my children; you will be very tired. If your cousins are departed they will have fine weather. Thy exercise is badly one; the master will blame thee. All (the) scholars will go to N. to-day. Charles, thou must wash thyself if thou wilt go with Henry. Yes, Mamma, I shall wash myself at present.

99.

Ich würde loben, I should or would praise;
du würdest loben, thou wouldst praise;
er würde loben, he would praise;
wir würden loben, we should praise;
ihr würdet loben, you would praise;
sie würden loben, they would praise.

Wenn ich hätte, if I had; wenn ich wäre, if I were; gern, willingly; ob, if.

Obs. After the conjunctions wenn and ob, if, the Subjunctive Mood is used in German, when the verb is in the Imperfect or in the Pluperfect tense.

Ich würde glücklicher sein, wenn ich Bücher und Freunde hätte. Ich würde mehr Vergnügen haben, wenn meine Vettern hier wären. Du würdest nicht so reich sein, wenn du nicht so viele Geschäfte gemacht hättest. Wenn Heinrich Geld hätte, würde er diese Messer kaufen. Ich würde deinen Bruder besuchen, wenn ich Zeit hätte. Du würdest diesen Hund nicht so sehr lieben, wenn er nicht so treu wäre. Wir würden dich nicht tadeln, wenn du fleißiger gewesen wärest. Dein Onkel sagte mir, du würdest morgen nicht kommen. Welchen von diesen Stöcken würdest du wählen? Wem würdet ihr eure Blumen geben? Was würdest du sagen, wenn ich meinen Hund verkaufte? Ich würde dir erlauben zu spielen, wenn du deine Aufgaben gemacht hättest. Diese Kinder würden sehr weinen, wenn ihre Mutter abgereist wäre. Dein Vater würde uns eine schöne Geschichte erzählen, wenn wir artiger gewesen wären. Wenn du Zeit zu lesen hättest, würde ich dir ein nützliches Buch leihen. Ich würde gern mit dir gehen, aber mein Lehrer will es nicht erlauben; ich muß heute noch drei Briefe schreiben.

100.

Louisa would be very (much) pleased if she had all these flowers. Henry would not have so many friends if he were not so kind (gut) and good (artig). We should not yet have (be) come if we had not received a letter from our father. We should not have sold our house if my father had done more business (pl.). The master would blame thee if thou hadst not done thy exercise. I should not believe it, if thou hadst not seen it. If we had an apple we should share it. We should go with you if we were not so tired. If I had some money I should buy a pound of cherries. If you loved me I should love you also. If you told me where Mr. N. lives, I would give you a glass of wine. Would you believe that I have done this? Would you do me this pleasure if I allowed you to play this evening? I would do it willingly if I had time.

101.

Ausgehen, to go out.
Ich gehe aus, I go out;

du gehst aus, thou goest out;
er geht aus, he goes out;
wir gehen aus, we go out;
ihr gehet aus, you go out;
sie gehen aus, they go out.

Aufmachen, to open;	abschreiben, to copy;
zumachen, to shut;	mittheilen, to communicate;
zurückschicken, to send back;	anziehen, to put on;
angenehm, pleasant;	schwarz, black;
die Nachricht, the news;	früher, earlier, sooner.

Obs. The compound verbs are formed by the addition of a particle which modifies the sense of the simple verb, and which is detached from it in the Present and Imperfect tenses of the Indicative Mood, unless the sentence begins with a conjunction or a relative pronoun.

Ich gehe heute nicht aus; das Wetter ist zu schlecht. Mein Bruder will auch nicht ausgehen. Wenn das Wetter schöner wäre, würden wir gern ausgehen. Heinrich, du machst nie die Thüre zu. Kannst du diese Kommode aufmachen? Ich mache mein Zimmer zu, wenn ich ausgehe. Ich schicke Ihnen diesen Abend das Buch zurück, welches Sie mir geliehen haben. Mein Vetter schickte mir gestern den Stock zurück, den ich ihm geliehen hatte. Schreibst du alle diese Briefe ab? Mußt du alles das abschreiben? Ich schreibe nur soviel ab als ich will. Ich würde diese Aufgabe noch abschreiben, wenn mein Lehrer es mir erlaubte. Ich muß Ihnen etwas mittheilen. Was wollen Sie mir mittheilen? Ich theil Ihnen eine angenehme Nachricht mit. Warum theilten Sie mir das nicht früher mit? Welches Kleid ziehst du heute an? Ich ziehe mein schwarzes Kleid an und meine Schwester wird ihr weißes Kleid anziehen. Wo ist das Kleid, welches Sie anziehen? Hier ist es.

102.

Die Gewohnheit, the habit;	aufstehen, to get up;
der Spaziergang, the walk;	weggehen, to go away;
einen Spaziergang machen, to take a walk.	

Do you not yet get up? No, I am indisposed; I shall not get up to-day. You always get up very late; that is a bad habit. I go away; I have much to do. I shall also go away. The weather is so fine that I have a mind to take a walk. Shut the door, if you please. Open the window. Your brother always opens the door and the windows. Do you not go out to-day? I shall not go out to-day. My father wishes (will) it not. My brother goes out twice every day. I shall send you back your umbrella to-morrow. Send me also back the cane which I have lent you. What is my son doing? He copies the letters which you have written this morning. My uncle is arrived; I shall communicate to him the good news. Put on your new dress; Mr. N. comes to see (visits) us to-day.

103.

Betrügen, to deceive;
beleidigen, to offend;
verlieren, to lose;
verbessern, to correct;
verbieten, to forbid;
erziehen, to bring up;
erhalten, to receive;
zerreißen, to tear;
warten, to wait;
anwenden, to employ;
zurückgeben, to give back;
die Gesellschaft, the company;
die Sorgfalt, the care;
sogleich, immediately, at once.

Obs. The syllables be, ge, ent, er, ver, and zer serve to form the *derived* verbs, and are not detached from the simple verb.

Dieser Kaufmann ist ein Betrüger, er betrügt Jedermann. Man muß Niemand betrügen. Wir betrügen Niemand. Du beleidigst mich immer. Dein Vetter beleidigte gestern die ganze Gesellschaft. Warum beleidigen Sie diesen Mann? Ich erhalte heute einen Brief von meinem Freunde in Köln. Wir erhalten alle Tage Nachricht von unserm Vater. Ich werde morgen Geld erhalten. Diese Mutter erzieht ihre Kinder mit vieler Sorgfalt. Wenn wir wollen, daß unsere Kinder gut werden, müssen wir sie mit Sorgfalt erziehen. Was suchst du, Karl? Ich habe meinen Ring verloren. Du verlierst immer etwas. Komm, wir müssen gehen, wir können nicht länger warten; du kannst den Ring später suchen. Gehen Sie nur, ich komme sogleich; ich werde den Ring finden. Warum zerreißest du dieses Papier? Das Papier ist mein, ich kann es zerreißen. Ich verbiete dir, es zu zerreißen. Willst du die Güte haben, mir meine Aufgaben zu verbessern? Dein Bruder verbesserte mir immer meine Aufgaben, als er noch hier war. Wann geben Sie mir meinen Bleistift zurück? Deine Brüder geben nie zurück, was man ihnen leiht. Wendet eure Zeit gut an. Man muß seine Zeit immer gut anwenden.

104.

I will not wait (any) longer. I lose my time. Shall you play to-day? No, we shall not play, we always lose. You would not lose if you played better. We should play better if we played oftener. If I receive my money I shall play once more (noch ein mal). Does your father not forbid you to play? No, he does not forbid (it) us. This child is very naughty; he tears his dresses. My neighbour brings up his children very badly. I do not like this young man; he always offends me. Henry corrects his exercise; he employs his time well. He who employs well his money is wise (weise). If you give me back my pencil, I shall give you back your pen. One must always give back what is lent us (what one lends us).

105.

Wohnen, to dwell; gewohnt, dwelt, been dwelling;
beleibigen, to offend; beleibigt, offended;
anwenden, to employ; angewendet, employed.

Obs. The Past Participle of simple verbs is formed by the addition of the initial syllable ge, and the final syllable et or t. In compound verbs ge is placed after the particle; the derived verbs take only the final et or t.

Haben Sie Ihre Aufgabe schon verbessert? Ich habe sie noch nicht verbessert; ich werde sie sogleich verbessern. Ihr Bruder hat mich gestern beleibigt; ich will nichts mehr mit ihm zu thun haben; von heute (an) ist er mein Freund nicht mehr. Wir wollen einen Spaziergang zusammen machen. Ich kann in diesem Augenblicke nicht ausgehen; ich habe diesen Morgen schon einen Spaziergang gemacht. Warum haben Sie mir mein Federmesser noch nicht zurückgegeben? Wer hat die Thüre aufgemacht? Wer hat Ihnen diese Nachricht mitgetheilt? Ihr Vater hat uns gestern eine artige Geschichte erzählt. Meine Mutter hat mir erlaubt, diesen Abend nach N. zu gehen. Sind Sie gestern bei meinem Vetter gewesen? Ja, wir haben den ganzen Tag bei ihm gespielt, gelacht und getanzt. Aber habt ihr auch gearbeitet? Ich glaube es nicht; der Lehrer hat dich schon mehrere male getadelt, deine Schwester hat es mir oft gesagt. Wer hat euch diesen Korb Kirschen geschickt? Hast du deinen kranken Freund noch nicht besucht? Mein Onkel hat ein neues Pferd gekauft; er hat das alte dem Kutscher unsers Nachbars für zwanzig Thaler verkauft.

106.

Einzig, single, only; nicht mehr, no more; Sache, Ding, thing.

Thou hast employed thy time very badly, my dear Henry. I see that thou hast not done a single exercise;

I have always praised thee, but I shall praise thee no more. Have you played together, my children? Yes, mamma, we have been playing and working. That is very well (gut); I shall give you some cherries and plums. I will divide them. We have divided them already. Why have you shut all (the) windows? The weather is so fine; I shall open them. Who has copied these letters? I believe that Henry has copied them. Have you been waiting long? We have waited (for) half an hour. Mr. N. has sent back the umbrella which you had lent him. I have received a letter from my aunt which I have not yet opened. Your cousin is arrived; he has told us (a) hundred things. One must not believe all that he tells. I have not believed all.

107.

Um . . . . . zu, in order to, to;
um zu loben, in order to praise, to praise;
um anzuwenden, in order to employ.

Wünschen, to wish; abreisen, to depart, set out; gefällig, obliging; sondern, but (after a negative phrase).

Obs. The preposition zu, which generally precedes the Infinitive, is placed in the compound verbs between the particle and the verb.

Ich komme, um dir zu sagen, daß ich morgen abreise. Ich habe meinen Bedienten geschickt, um mir ein Pfund Zucker zu kaufen. Wir leben nicht, um zu essen, sondern wir essen, um zu leben. Um glücklich zu sein, muß man zufrieden sein. Um Freunde zu haben, muß man gefällig sein. Ich habe nicht Zeit, auszugehen. Haben Sie die Güte, diese zwei Briefe abzuschreiben. Wollen Sie so gut sein, die Thüre aufzumachen? Wir haben Lust, einen kleinen Spaziergang zu machen. Mein Nachbar hat zwei Pferde zu verkaufen. Wer hat dir erlaubt, so früh wegzugehen? Ist es noch nicht Zeit, aufzustehen? Ich habe das Vergnügen gehabt, den Herrn Moll zu sehen. Wünschen Sie mit meinem Vater zu sprechen? Ich wünsche mit ihrer Frau Mutter zu sprechen. Haben Sie Geld, um diesen Ring zu kaufen? Hast du Zeit, mir meine Aufgabe zu verbessern? Hat dein Vater dir dieses Geld gegeben, um es so schlecht anzuwenden?

108.

Das Unglück, the misfortune; der Gegenstand, the subject.

It is no subject for laughter (in order to laugh). It is very difficult. I have had the pleasure to dance with

Miss N. Mr. Nollet has had the kindness to lend me his horse. Do you wish to go out with me? I have no time to go to N. We have much to do to-day. My brother has six letters to copy. I have good news to communicate to you. Have the kindness to send me back my book. It is time to set out. Which dress do you wish to put on? Allow me to open the window, it is so warm. I am come to see if you are well (wohl). I am very (much) indisposed; I have too much to do. You have the bad habit to get up too late. A young man must get up earlier. My friend has had the misfortune to lose his parents. I come to bring you your boots. That is very well (gut). I had no mind to wait (any) longer.

109.

Ich werde geliebt, I am loved;
du wirst geliebt,
er wird geliebt,
wir werden geliebt,
ihr werdet geliebt,
sie werden geliebt.

Ich wurde geliebt, I was loved;
du wurdest geliebt,
er wurde geliebt,
wir wurden geliebt,
ihr wurdet geliebt,
sie wurden geliebt.

Belohnen, to reward; strafen, to punish; achten, to esteem; verachten, to despise; geschickt, clever; unwissend, ignorant.

Obs. The verb werden constructed with the past participle forms the passive voice. Thus the verb *to be* is translated by werden when the subject is sensible of a certain action; and by sein when he finds himself in a certain condition. *I am paid*, in the sense of *they pay me*, is expressed by, ich werde bezahlt; but in the sense of *they have paid me*, it is expressed by, ich bin bezahlt.

Ich werde von meinem Vater gelobt, wenn ich fleißig und artig bin. Du wirst von deinem Lehrer getadelt, weil du immer faul bist. Heinrich wird gestraft, weil er unartig ist. Welcher Mann wird gelobt und welcher wird getadelt? Der geschickte Mann wird gelobt und der unwissende getadelt. Welche Knaben werden belohnt und welche werden gestraft? Diejenigen, welche fleißig sind, werden belohnt und die, welche faul sind, gestraft. Wir werden von unsern Aeltern geliebt; ihr werdet von den eurigen getadelt. Meine Brüder werden von Jedermann geachtet. Wir werden von unsern Feinden verachtet. Wird dieses Kind nie gestraft? Von wem werdet ihr gelobt? Deine Schwester wird von ihrer Mutter getadelt, weil sie nicht arbeitet. Ich wurde immer von meinem Lehrer geliebt und gelobt, weil ich fleißig und artig war. Heinrich wurde immer von seinem Vater gestraft, wenn er nicht arbeitete.

110.

Ich bin geliebt worden, I have been loved;
du bist geliebt worden,
er ist geliebt worden,
wir sind geliebt worden,
ihr seid geliebt worden,
sie sind geliebt worden.

Tödten, to kill; erfunden, invented; entdeckt, discovered; die Mühe, the trouble, pains; das Pulver, gunpowder; mehrere, several.

Ich bin von meinem Vater gestraft worden, weil ich diese Briefe nicht abgeschrieben habe. Du bist von deinem Onkel belohnt worden, weil du seine Uhr gefunden hast. Heinrich ist für seine Mühe nicht belohnt worden. Diese Nachricht ist uns durch Herrn Moll mitgetheilt worden. Von wem ist diese Aufgabe verbessert worden? Wir sind von diesem Menschen mehrere male beleidigt worden. Diese Herren sind gestern in der Gesellschaft sehr getadelt worden. Dieses Kind ist von seiner Mutter gewaschen worden. Es ist mir gesagt worden, daß Sie einen Bedienten suchten. Von wem sind diese Kinder geschickt worden? Diese Häuser sind gestern alle verkauft worden. Wir sind oft von unserm Lehrer gelobt worden, weil wir immer unsere Aufgaben machten. Gustav Adolf ist bei Lützen getödtet worden. Das Pulver ist von Berthold Schwarz erfunden worden. Amerika ist von Columbus entdeckt worden.

111.

Sich freuen, to rejoice.

Ich freue mich, I rejoice;
du freust dich,
er freut sich,
wir freuen uns,
ihr freuet euch,
sie freuen sich.

Ich habe mich gefreut, I have rejoiced;
du hast dich gefreut,
er hat sich gefreut,
wir haben uns gefreut,
ihr habt euch gefreut,
sie haben sich gefreut.

Sich irren, to be mistaken; sich befinden, to be, to do; sich wundern, to be astonished; sich ankleiden, to dress (one's self); sich unterhalten, to be amused; danken, to thank; zweifeln, to doubt; wiedersehen, to see again; selten, seldom; auf, on, upon.

Guten Tag, lieber Heinrich. Ich freue mich, dich wiederzusehen. Wie geht es? Wie befindest du dich? Ich danke dir, ich befinde mich sehr wohl, seit ich auf dem Lande wohne. Was macht dein Bruder? Ist er wohl? Ja, er befindet sich sehr wohl. Was thust du, Ludwig? Ich kleide mich an. Kleidet ihr euch noch nicht an? Wir werden uns später ankleiden. Haben Sie sich schon gewaschen, Henriette? Ich habe mich noch nicht gewaschen, aber meine Schwester hat sich schon gewaschen. Ist das mein Bruder, der da mit dem Herrn N. kommt? Sie irren sich, es ist nicht Ihr Bruder. Ich glaube nicht, daß ich mich irre. Ich irre mich selten. Ich habe mich noch nie geirrt. Wir gehen diesen Abend nach N. Ich zweifle nicht, daß wir uns gut unterhalten werden. Wie haben Sie sich gestern in dem Concert unterhalten? Sehr gut, Herr N. hat sehr gut gespielt. Ich wundere mich, daß Sie nicht da waren. Ich hatte noch Vieles zu thun; ich habe bis zehn Uhr gearbeitet.

112.

Art thou not yet dressed, Charles? I shall dress myself at present. Why hast thou not yet dressed thyself? I had still two exercises to do. I rejoice to see that thou art so diligent. I love him who rejoices when his friend is praised. I saw your brother yesterday. You are mistaken; my brother is no longer here. I am not mistaken; I have seen him with his friend Ferdinand. Why have you not washed yourself? I should have washed myself if I had had any water. We were in the country yesterday; we have been very much amused. How does your sister do? She is very well since she has been (is) with her uncle. And how have you been since I saw you? I have been very well. I am astonished that you are not yet departed. I shall set out this evening.

113.

Es regnet, it rains;	es freut mich, I am glad, happy;
es schneit, it snows;	es thut mir leid, I am sorry;
es hagelt, it hails;	es ist mir kalt, I am cold;
es blitzt, it lightens;	es ist mir warm, I am warm;
es donnert, it thunders;	es hungert mich, I am hungry;
es friert, it freezes;	es durstet mich, I am thirsty.

Befehlen, to command; bleiben, to stay; erwarten, to expect; zu Mittag essen, to dine; leben Sie wohl, farewell, adieu.

Regnet es? Nein, es regnet nicht. Es regnete, als ich gekommen bin. Es hat die ganze Nacht geregnet. Es wird morgen gewiß regnen. Ich glaube, daß es schneit. Hat es geschneit? Wenn es schneite, würde es nicht regnen. Es wird diese Nacht frieren, denn es ist sehr kalt. Ich muß ausgehen, aber es hagelt, wie ich sehe. Mir ist sehr warm: es blitzt, sogleich wird es donnern. Wir wollen nach Hause gehen. Es freut mich, daß ich Sie finde; aber es thut mir leid, daß ich nicht mit Ihnen gehen kann. Mein Onkel ist gestern Abend angekommen und wünscht, daß wir heute bei ihm zu Mittag essen. Haben Sie nichts zu trinken, mich durstet sehr. Wünschen Sie ein Glas Bier oder Wasser? Sie haben nur zu befehlen; hier ist, was Sie wünschen. Aber mich hungert auch; geben Sie mir ein Stück Schinken und ein wenig Brot. Sie haben da schöne Birnen und Pflaumen. Es gibt dieses Jahr viel Obst. Wollen Sie heute bei uns bleiben? Ich danke Ihnen, ich habe meinem Vetter versprochen, heute mit ihm nach S. zu gehen; er wird mich gewiß schon erwarten. Leben Sie wohl.

114.

Was für Wetter ist es? What kind of weather is it?

What sort of weather is it? It is bad weather; it is raining (it rains). It did not rain when you came. It will rain the whole day. It has been raining this morning. Does it snow? No, it does not snow. It would snow if it were colder. I believe that it freezes. The weather is finer to-day; it is warm. I am very warm. It has lightened; it will thunder later. I am sorry that you are not come sooner. Art thou hungry? Yes, I am hungry and thirsty. I have taken (made) a long walk. I shall drink a glass of wine if you (will) allow it. My sister will be happy to see you again. She has often spoken of you to me. Will your nephew come also? I doubt whether he will come (comes). He has too much to do.

115.

Wie viel Uhr ist es?	What o'clock is it?
es ist sechs Uhr;	it is six o'clock;
es ist halb sieben;	it is half past six;
es ist ein Viertel auf sieben;	it is a quarter past six.

Aufstehen, to get up; schlafen gehen, to go to bed; ausruhen, to repose; spazieren, spazieren gehen, to go to walk; zu Abend essen, to sup.

Um wie viel Uhr stehen Sie gewöhnlich auf? Ich stehe jeden Morgen um sechs Uhr auf und gehe um zehn Uhr schlafen. Sind Sie spazieren gewesen? Ja, ich habe eine Stunde in dem Walde spaziert. Ich bin sehr müde, ich will ein wenig ausruhen Wie viel Uhr ist es? Es ist acht Uhr; es ist noch nicht halb neun. Um wie viel Uhr sind Sie angekommen? Ich bin um ein Viertel auf sechs angekommen. Meine Schwester ist um drei Viertel auf acht abgereist. Wie lange bleiben Sie hier? Ich werde nur zwei bis drei Tage bleiben. Um wie viel Uhr essen wir zu Mittag? Ich glaube um zwölf Uhr oder um halb eins. Um drei Uhr trinken wir Kaffee und um sieben Uhr essen wir zu Abend.

116.

Zahlreich, numerous; vor, before; nach Hause, home.

Have the kindness to tell me what o'clock it is, It is not yet eleven o'clock; it is half past ten. I must depart at twelve o'clock, or at half past twelve. Have you already dined? No, I shall dine with my cousin; we dine generally at two o'clock. At what o'clock do you sup? I shall sup at nine o'clock. Have you a mind to walk a little? If it does not rain, I shall walk a little with you. It is fine weather; we will go to N., we shall find there a numerous party (Gesellschaft). Are you already tired? I am very tired; it is too warm. If you allow (it), I will repose a little. Get up; it is time to go home. I must go to bed before ten o'clock, in order to get up to-morrow at five o'clock.

117.

Acc.	Dat.	Dat. et Acc.
Für, for;	aus, out of;	an, at, of;
durch, by; through;	mit, with;	auf, upon, on;
ohne, without;	nach, to, after;	in, in, into;
gegen, to, towards, against;	von, from;	unter, under.

Friedrich, Frederic; der Markt, the market; der Wille, the will, der Keller, the cellar; die Küche, the kitchen; die Kirche, the church; legen, to put, lay; sitzen, to sit; denken, to think; wo, where; wohin, whereto; woher, wherefrom.

Obs. The prepositions an, auf, in, unter, govern the Accusative when the verb of the phrase denotes a movement or a direction towards an object; and the Dative, when it does not express this movement.

Für wen sind diese Bücher? Dieses ist für mich und jenes ist für meine Schwester. Wo ist der junge Mann, für den Sie alle diese Sachen gekauft haben? Durch welche Straße müssen wir gehen, um auf den Markt zu kommen?

Durch die Friedrichsstraße oder die Wilhelmsstraße? Gehen Sie ohne Regenschirm aus? Es wird sogleich regnen. Was ist das Leben ohne einen Freund? Ich kann ohne dich nicht leben. Du bist gegen den Willen deines Vaters ausgegangen. Warum ist dein Bruder immer gegen mich? Woher kommst du? Ich komme vom Spaziergange, aus der Schule, aus der Kirche. Die Magd kommt aus dem Keller, aus dem Garten, aus der Küche. Mit wem seid ihr ausgegangen? Mit dem Onkel, mit der Tante, mit Ihnen. Nach dem Essen gehen wir aus. Wann kommen Sie zurück? Kommen Sie vor oder nach uns zurück? Wir werden nach Ihnen zurückkommen. Wo ist meine Schwester? Sie ist in der Kirche, in dem Garten, auf dem Markte. Wohin geht deine Mutter? Sie geht in die Küche, in den Keller, auf den Markt. Wohin hast du mein Buch gelegt? Ich habe es auf den Tisch, unter den Stuhl gelegt. Wo ist die kleine Luise? Sie sitzt auf dem Stuhle, unter dem Tische, an der Thüre. Schreiben Sie an Ihren Vetter oder an Ihre Base? An wen denken Sie? Ich denke an die arme Frau, welche ich gestern bei Ihnen gesehen habe.

118.

Der Schrank, the press; undankbar, ungrateful.

This is for me, that is for you. He who is not for me is against me. I cannot do this without him, without her, without you. I shall arrive before you; you will arrive after me. You are ungrateful towards us. I always think of you, but you never think of me. There is thy little sister; hast thou nothing for her? You do not love my brother, you are always against him. Where is your son? This fruit and these flowers are for him. Where have you been? We have been at (in the) church and at (in the) school. Where are you going? We are going into the garden, to (on the) market, into the kitchen. Where do these children come from? They come from the public walk (Spaziergang), from church, from the garden. Where have you put my stockings and shoes? I have put them on your chair, on the table in the press. Have you seen my brother? I have seen him at the public walk, in the garden, at the door. I write to my uncle and aunt. We often speak of him and of her.

119.

Im instead of in dem;	am	instead of	an dem;
ins , , in das;	ans	,	, an das;
zum , , zu dem;	vom	,	, von dem;
zur , , zu der;	unterm	,	, unter dem.

Das Feuer, the fire; sich stellen, to place one's self, to stand.

Obs. The quickness of the pronunciation has introduced the custom of contracting the definite article with certain prepositions.

Die Magd ist im Keller oder im Garten. Wir gehen diesen Abend ins Theater oder ins Concert. Schicken Sie den Bedienten zum Schuhmacher oder zum Schneider? Gehen wir heute zur Tante oder bleiben wir zu Hause? Waren Sie gestern bei dem Minister? Kommen Sie zu mir oder zu meinem Bruder? Warum sitzen Sie immer beim Feuer? Ist Ihnen so kalt? Was haben Sie am Auge, am Fuße? Warum tragen Sie eine Feder am Hute? Stellen Sie sich an die Thüre oder ans Fenster. Haben Sie diese Blume vom Gärtner erhalten? Sie arbeiten vom Morgen bis zum Abend. Was machen Sie unterm Tische? Ich suche meine Bleifeder. Karl hat sie ins Schreibzeug gelegt.

120.

Wovon, of what;	davon, of that, of it;
womit, with what;	damit, with that, with it;
wozu, for what;	dazu, for that, for it;
woran, at what;	daran, at that, at it;
worin, in what;	darin, in that, in it;
wodurch, by what;	dadurch, by that, by it.

Herab, hinab, down;
herauf, hinauf, up;
herein, hinein, in.

Brauchen, to use; gesprochen, spoken; gedacht, thought; ging, went; fiel, fell; das Klavier, the piano.

Obs. 1) All these particles are formed of prepositions, combined with the adverbs wo, da, her and hin. If, in the formation of these words, two vowels meet, an r is inserted, to avoid the hiatus. 2) Her denotes a movement towards the person speaking; hin, a movement from the speaker.

Wovon sprechen Sie? Ist dies das Buch, wovon Sie sprechen? Womit haben Sie das gemacht? Ist das die Feder, womit Sie diesen Brief geschrieben haben? Wozu brauchen Sie das? Woran denken Sie denn? Ist das das Haus, worin ihr Onkel wohnt, die Stadt, wodurch Sie gekommen sind? Hat man von meinem Unglück gesprochen? Ja, man hat davon gesprochen. Haben Sie an meine Sache gedacht? Nein, ich habe nicht daran gedacht. Sind Sie mit Ihrem neuen Klavier zufrieden? Nein, ich bin nicht zufrieden damit. Ist noch Wein in der Flasche? Nein, es ist keiner mehr darin. Wie viel Ellen müssen Sie zu einem neuen Rocke haben? Ich muß drei und eine halbe Elle dazu haben. Kommen Sie herauf. Gehen Sie hinab, hinunter. Warum kommen Sie nicht herein? Warum gehen Sie nicht hinein? Der Knabe ging zu nah' ans Wasser und fiel hinein. Werden Sie diesen Abend ins Theater gehen? Wir werden nicht hingehen, aber Heinrich und Karl gehen hin.

121.

Bitten, to beg, to ask; der Krieg, the war; das Schauspiel, the play.

Do you know of what I speak, of what I think? That is not the same street, through which we came (are come) this morning, the same house where we were yesterday. Do you speak of (the) war? Yes, we speak of it. Do you think of the concert? We do not think of it. Are you pleased with this ring? I am very (much) pleased with it. Why do you not come up? Tell your brother that I am coming down directly. Come in, my friends. I beg you to come in. Do you go to the play this evening? We shall not go there. Do you know where this gentleman lives, where he goes to, and where he is? We do not know it.

122.

Der Tisch, the table; das Tischchen, the little table. Die Taube, the pigeon; pflanzen, to plant; eben, soeben, just now, just.

Obs. Diminutives are formed by adding the syllable chen, and softening the radical vowel. If the primitive word ends in e or en, this termination is omitted.

Amalie hat ihr Hütchen verloren. Wir haben drei hübsche Bäumchen gepflanzt. Wem gehört dieses artige Gärtchen? Wie viel hast du für dieses Täubchen bezahlt? Wohin gehen diese Herrchen? Komm, Luischen, wir wollen zu der Tante gehen, sie hat ein neues Kätzchen und ein neues Hündchen. Ich habe eben ein Briefchen von meiner Schwester erhalten, worin sie mich bittet, ihr ein Messerchen und ein Löffelchen zu kaufen. Ich will recht artig sein, Mütterchen, wenn du mir ein neues Kleidchen kaufst. Trage dieses Tischchen in den Garten, Henriette, wir wollen ein Stündchen darin arbeiten. Welches Dörfchen sehe ich ca unten im Walde? Welches Kind hat diese Schühchen verloren? Friedrich hat ein artiges Vögelchen vom Gärtner erhalten. Wem gehören alle diese Blümchen? Wo ist dein Schwesterchen, Johann?

123.

Nöthig haben, to want; sich schämen, to be ashamed of; pflegen, to use, to be in the habit of; schläfrig, sleepy; Durst haben, to be thirsty; der Spaziergang, the walk, the public walk; scheinen, to shine; früh, early; spät, late; ich möchte, I should like.

Heinrich, hast du Lust einen Spaziergang mit mir zu machen? Ich habe keine Lust, jetzt auszugehen. Ich bin schläfrig. Schämst du dich nicht, so faul zu sein? Komm, wir wollen in den Garten meines Onkels gehen. Wie viel Uhr ist es? Es ist erst sechs Uhr, die Sonne scheint noch. Du hast Recht, es ist noch früh, ich will mit dir gehen. Ich pflege jeden Abend einen Spaziergang zu machen, ehe ich zu Bette gehe. Das ist eine gute Gewohnheit. Es ist mir aber sehr warm; wir gehen zu geschwind. Ich habe großen Durst, ich möchte einmal trinken. Wenn man warm ist, muß man nicht trinken. Ich habe nöthig, ein wenig auszuruhen; ich bin so müde, daß ich nicht mehr fort kann. Du mußt einen Augenblick Geduld haben. Komm, ich fürchte zu spät nach Hause zu kommen.

124.

To have patience, Geduld haben; to fear, fürchten; to be hardhearted, hartherzig sein; to have the head-ache, Kopfweh haben, to take pains, sich bemühen; the moment, der Augenblick; some pretext, ein Vorwand (masc.); directly, sogleich; the advice, der Rath.

How, you are still in bed? Are you not ashamed to sleep so long? I should be ashamed to get up so late. I cannot get up to-day, I have the head-ache. You are a little idler (Faulenzer). When you must go to school, you always look for some pretext. You are in the habit of going to bed early and getting up late. That is a bad habit. I beg you to have patience (for) a moment. I shall get up directly. I have no mind to wait (any) longer. I fear to come to church too late. You are very hard-hearted: you have no pity for a poor patient (der Kranke). You are not ill; you have no mind to go to school. You are right, my friend; I shall take pains to get rid of this fault (diesen Fehler abzulegen) and to follow your good advice.

125.

Glauben, to believe.

I believe that it is already late. We do not believe it. Neither does my brother believe it. Do you believe it? I do not believe it. If I did believe it, you would laugh. I have never believed this. Who would have believed that? I should believe it if you told me so (it me). It is an incredible thing. You would believe it indeed if you saw it. These gentlemen do not believe it. How will you have me (that I should) believe it? Your brother believed every thing that was told him (all that one told him); he was too credulous. He would not believe it if he knew you.

Neither, auch nicht; laugh, lachen; would have, hätte; incredible, unglaublich; indeed, wohl; saw, sähen; credulous, leichtgläubig; knew, kennte.

126.

Sagen, to say, to tell.

I have something to tell you. What have you to say to me? I tell you nothing. Tell (it) me only. I shall tell you another time. You will not tell my brother what I have written to you. Do not tell him that I am still in bed. What has he told you? Have I not told it you? You have not yet told (it) me. Do you wish (will you) me to (that I) tell it? One must not tell everything that one knows. He has told it me in a whisper. Your uncle told me yesterday that he would sell his house. What do you say to that? I would tell you with pleasure, if I knew it. If I said otherwise I should lie.

Only, nur; knows, weiß; in a whisper, ins Ohr; if I knew, wenn ich wüßte; otherwise, anders; lie, lügen.

127.

Wünschen, to wish; hoffen, to hope.

I wish that your enterprise may succeed. We often wish (for) things which are hurtful to us. I should wish to be able to serve you. I hope that our friend will obtain the situation that he wishes (to get). She did hope to win her law-suit, but she was mistaken. My cousin has nothing more to hope. We hope everything of Providence. My sister hopes that you will do what you have promised her. Never wish (for) what you cannot have. What do you wish? (For) what do you hope? I believe that my father will arrive to-day. We must hope it. These gentlemen wish that we should depart. Does your sister wish to go with us?

May succeed, gelingen; hurtful, schädlich; to be able, können; to serve, dienen, nützlich sein; obtain, erhalten; situation, Stelle (fem.); win, gewinnen; law-suit, Proceß: Providence, Vorsehung (fem.); for what, worauf

128.

Schreiben, to write; ich schrieb, I wrote; geschrieben, written.
lesen, to read; ich las, I read; gelesen, read.

I am writing a letter to my brother. My mother will write to him to-morrow. You wrote better formerly. What have you written to him? Have you not yet written to him that our friend Henry is dead? Write that to him. If I had a good pen I should write also. You write too fast; write more slowly. Show me what you have written. You must write once more. What do you read? I read an amusing book. What didst thou read yesterday when thou wast with thy uncle? I read the fables of Gellert, which are very well written. We should read oftener if we had more time. How must we (one) read this word? Remember well what you have read. Would you like (will you) me to (that I should) read this letter to you? I should like to know how to read like you.

Formerly, früher, sonst; fast, schnell; slowly, langsam; show, zeigen; once more, noch einmal; amusing, unterhaltend; fable, Fabel (fem.); remember, behalten; I should like to know how, ich möchte können; like, wie.

129.

Sehen, to see; ich sah, I saw; gesehen, seen;
kennen, to know; ich kannte, I knew; gekannt, known.

What do I see? Do you not see it? I see nothing. Do but look. It is well worth the trouble, to see it. I saw your cousin yesterday. Have you not seen him? Do you see how I do this? Your cousin does not see me. If I saw my friend I should tell him that you are here. Would you like (will you) me to (that I) bring (a) light; or can you see still? I have seen Mr. N. to-day. Does he know me? I believe that he knows you. He has greeted me. Have you also known my uncle? Have you not told me that you knew him? I should know him again if I saw him. Your brother has recognized me by my voice. These children do not know me (any) more.

Do look, sehen Sie doch einmal; well worth the trouble, wohl der Mühe werth; to greet, grüßen; to know again, to recognize, wiedererkennen; by the voice, an der Stimme.

130.

Gehen, to go; ich ging, I went; gegangen, gone;
weggehen, to go away; ausgehen, to go out.

Where are you going? I am going to my aunt, and my brother goes to school. Where did you go this morning with your cousin? We went to church. I should willingly go to walk if you would go with me. I shall go with you, but do not go so fast. Where is your sister? She is gone to see her uncle. We should have gone together if I had had time. Shall you not go to N. to-morrow? My father does not wish (will not) me to (that I should) go there. I go away. Do you go away already? Henry does not yet go away. William is already gone away. Go away. I must go away. I believe that your friends are gone away already. At what o'clock do you go out? I go out every morning at seven o'clock. And at what o'clock dost thou go out? I went out yesterday at six o'clock. Is your brother already gone out? To-morrow I shall go out early. I must go out at half past one. My mother did not wish (would not) that I should go out (went out).

To go to walk, spazieren gehen; to go to see any one, zu Jemandem gehen.

131.

Kommen, to come; ich kam, I came; gekommen, come;
zurückkommen, to come back; ankommen, to arrive.

Whence do you come so late? We come out of the garden. Eliza does not come to-day; she is gone into the country with her father. Come to see me this afternoon. It is possible that I may come. I should wish that you came early. Formerly you came every day. I should come oftener if I had not so much to do. My brother is not yet come back. He will come back this evening. My uncle does not come back (any) more. We saw your uncle when we came back from the country. At what o'clock does the post arrive? I believe it arrives at three o'clock. Yesterday it came very late. Formerly it arrived at two o'clock. My sisters will arrive to-day from Liége.

Eliza, Elise; to come to see, besuchen; afternoon, Nachmittag; possible, möglich; evening, Abend; the post, die Post; Liége, Lüttich.

132.

Trinken, to drink; ich trank, I drank; getrunken, drunk; austrinken, to finish (a glass, a cup, etc.); essen, to eat; ich aß, I ate; gegessen, eaten; zu Mittag essen, to dine.

Have you nothing to drink? I drink no wine. We drink only water, and my brother drinks beer. You do not drink. I have the honor to drink your health. When I was young, I drank nothing but (only) milk. This gentleman has drunk a little too much. He does not eat much, but he drinks much. Who has drunk out of my glass? I will drink no more. We will drink another glass. The wine which we drank yesterday was so good that every one drank a bottle. Finish your glass. You have not yet finished your glass. Drink again. Have you no appetite? Eat a little ham. I have eaten enough, I have no more appetite. You will eat another piece of meat. This child eats the whole day. We ate some days ago (some) delicious fish. At what o'clock do you dine? I dine generally at two o'clock, but to-day I dine at four o'clock. After dinner I drink a cup of coffee and then I go out to walk.

To your health, auf Ihre Gesundheit; the honor, die Ehre; another glass, noch ein Glas; every one, Jeder; again, noch einmal; the appetite, der Appetit; some days ago, vor einigen Tagen; delicious fish, köstliche Fische; the dinner, das Mittagsessen; then, dann.

133.

Können, to be able, to know; ich konnte, I could; gekonnt, been able; wissen, to know; ich wußte, I knew; gewußt, known.

Can you tell me what o'clock it is? I cannot tell (it) you, I have not (got) my watch with me. If I had it with me I could tell you exactly. I shall not be able to go out to-day; my father is ill. My brother will not be able to come. I should wish, however, that he could come. I should be able to lend you this book if it belonged to me. Lewis can carry this letter to the post-office. I could not go out yesterday. My friend could not answer your letter, because he had too much to do. Do you know when my father will come back? I do not know. Does your sister know it? We know all that we must die. Do you know (how) to dance? I have known it, but I do not know it (any) more. My father knew several languages. Henry can speak German. These boys know neither how to read nor how to write. The men do not know (how) to employ their time. I did not know that your rother was departed. I shall soon know who has one that. How can you suppose (will you) that I hould know this? I should wish that you knew it. (I would, etc.)

Exactly, genau; however, jedoch; I should wish, ich wollte; to belong, gehören; answer, antworten auf (Acc.); because, weil; to dance, tanzen; to speak German, beutsch sprechen.

134.

Thun, to do; ich that, I did; gethan, done;
nehmen, to take; ich nahm, I took; genommen, taken.

What are you doing? I do what you have ordered me (to do). What were you doing when I came in? I was lighting the fire. What will you do this evening? I shall do nothing this evening. Your brother does nothing but run. These children do nothing but drink and eat. When one has done one's duty, one has nothing to reproach one's self (with). You have done a good action. Why are you in bad spirits? What have they done to you? One must do the will of God. You will write to him; in your place I should not do it. I shall do my best to satisfy him. I take this for myself. How many books do you take? Your brother always takes my pen. Will you take my place? Take what you wish. Take this child by the hand. Who has taken my copy-book? Your cousin took my cane yesterday. I shall take one of these apples, if you allow (it). I have taken the liberty to write to him. We took some chairs and we sat down. If I took these books, my father would scold me.

To order, befehlen; to come in, hereinkommen; to light, anzünden; nothing but, nichts als; one's duty, seine Pflicht; to reproach one's self, sich verwerfen; action, Handlung, That; in bad spirits, übler Laune; in your place, an Ihrer Stelle; to do one's best, sein Möglichstes thun; to satisfy befriedigen; myself, mich; place, Platz (m.); by the hand, bei der Hand; liberty, Freiheit; to sit down, sich setzen; to scold any one, mit Jemandem schmälen.

135.

Schlafen, to sleep; ich schlief, I slept; geschlafen, slept; brechen, zerbrechen, to break; ich brach, I broke; gebrochen, broken.

We sleep too much; you sleep less than we. I sleep generally (for) seven hours. Formerly I slept longer. My brother slept yesterday till eight o'clock; but to-morrow he will not sleep so long, because he must depart for Cologne at four o'clock. Our mother does not allow us to sleep longer than till six o'clock. I sleep soundly. You were very uneasy in your sleep last night. This child sleeps very peaceably. We have no knife to cut our bread; therefore we break it. You will break this stick if you bend it so. I do not believe that it (will) break. I should not like it to (that it did) break. This boy has broken a pane. He broke two last week. This servant is very heedless; she breaks something every day. Yesterday she broke two glasses, and on Sunday half a dozen cups and saucers.

Less, weniger; soundly, sehr fest; to be uneasy in one's sleep, unruhig schlafen; last, vorig; peaceably, sanft; to cut, schneiden; therefore, deshalb; to bend, beugen; I should not like, ich möchte nicht; pane, Scheibe; heedless, unbedacht; on Sunday, am Sonntag; cups and saucers, Tassen.

136.

Rathen, to advise; ich rieth, I advised; gerathen, advised; bringen, to bring; ich brachte, I brought; gebracht, brought; empfehlen, to recommend; ich empfahl, I recommended; empfohlen, recommended.

I do not know what to resolve; what do you advise me to do? One advises me this, the other that. They advised me yesterday to give up a part of my rights. I should like you to advise (that you advised) me; in you I have the greatest confidence. Because you wish me to advise (that I advise) you, I tell you that the most unprofitable accommodation is better than the most favorable law-suit. I shall bring you the fruits which you desire (to have). I believe they have brought them to me already. They brought me yesterday some letters from Berlin. When you come back, bring your sister with (you). Mr. N. will bring his son with (him) to-morrow. They brought their aunt with (them) from Vienna. I should wish you to bring (that you brought) the young man with (you) of whom you have spoken. He recommends his son to me. You recommended your business to him. I have recommended him to watch over him.

What to resolve, wozu ich mich entschließen soll; one, they, man; even, sogar; to give up, abtreten; the right, das Recht; I should like, ich wollte; in you, zu Ihnen; the greatest confidence, das meiste Zutrauen; the most unprofitable accommodation etc., ein magerer Vergleich ist besser als ein fetter Proceß; to desire, wünschen; the business, das Geschäft; to watch, wachen; over, über.

Exercises for reading.

1. *The little dog.*

Ein Fräulein, mit Namen Karoline, ging einst an dem Ufer eines Flusses spazieren. Sie begegnete hier einigen bösen Knaben, die ein Hündchen ertränken wollten; sie hatte Mitleid mit dem armen Thiere, kaufte es und nahm es mit sich auf das Schloß.

Das Hündchen hatte bald mit seiner neuen Gebieterin Bekanntschaft gemacht und verließ sie keinen Augenblick mehr. Eines Abends, als sie sich zu Bette legen wollte, fing das Hündchen plötzlich an zu bellen. Karoline nahm das Licht, sah unter das Bett und erblickte einen Menschen von fürchterlichem Aussehen, der sich hier verborgen hatte. Es war ein Dieb.

Karoline rief um Hülfe und alle Bewohner des Schlosses eilten auf ihr Geschrei herbei. Sie ergriffen den Räuber und überlieferten ihn der Gerechtigkeit. Er gestand in seinem Verhöre, daß es seine Absicht gewesen wäre, das Fräulein zu ermorden und das Schloß zu plündern.

Karoline dankte dem Himmel, daß er sie so glücklich gerettet habe, und sagte: Niemand hätte geglaubt, daß das arme Thierchen, dem ich das Leben gerettet habe, mir auch das meinige retten würde.

2. *The good neighbours.*

Der kleine Knabe eines Müllers näherte sich zu sehr dem Bache und fiel hinein. Der Schmied, welcher jenseit des Baches wohnte, sah es, sprang in das Wasser, zog das Kind heraus und brachte es dem Vater.

Ein Jahr darauf brach während der Nacht Feuer in der Schmiede aus. Das Haus stand ganz in Flammen, ehe der Schmied es merkte. Er rettete sich mit Frau und Kindern. Nur sein kleinstes Töchterchen hatte man im ersten Schrecken vergessen.

Das Kind fing in dem brennenden Hause an zu schreien; allein kein Mensch wollte sich hinein wagen. Da kam plötzlich der Müller, sprang in die Flammen, brachte das Kind glücklich heraus, gab es dem Schmied in die Arme und sagte:

Gott sei gelobt, daß er mir Gelegenheit gab, Euch meine Dankbarkeit zu beweisen. Ihr habt meinen Sohn aus dem Wasser gezogen und ich habe mit Gottes Hülfe Eure Tochter aus dem Feuer errettet.

3. *The broken horse-shoe.*

Ein Bauer ging mit seinem Sohne, dem kleinen Thomas, in die Stadt. Sieh, sagte er unterwegs zu ihm, da liegt ein Stück von einem Hufeisen an der Erde, hebe es auf und stecke es in die Tasche. Bah, versetzte Thomas, das ist nicht der Mühe werth, daß man sich dafür bückt. Der Vater erwiderte nichts, nahm das Eisen und steckte es in seine Tasche. Im nächsten Dorfe verkaufte er es dem Schmiede für drei Heller und kaufte dafür Kirschen.

Hierauf setzten sie ihren Weg fort. Die Sonne war brennend heiß. Man sah weit und breit weder Haus, noch Wald, noch Quelle. Thomas verging vor Durst und konnte seinem Vater nur mit Mühe folgen.

Da ließ dieser, wie durch Zufall, eine Kirsche fallen. Thomas hob sie so gierig auf, als wäre es Gold, und steckte sie schnell in den Mund. Einige Schritte weiter ließ der Vater eine zweite Kirsche fallen, welche Thomas mit derselben Gierigkeit ergriff. Dies dauerte fort, bis er sie alle aufgehoben hatte.

Als er die letzte verzehrt hatte, wandte der Vater sich zu ihm hin und sagte: Sieh, wenn du dich ein einziges mal hättest bücken wollen, um das Hufeisen aufzuheben, so würdest du nicht nöthig gehabt haben, es hundert mal für die Kirschen zu thun.

4. *The hidden treasure.*

Kurz vor seinem Tode sagte ein Bauer zu seinen drei Söhnen: Liebe Kinder, ich kann euch nichts hinterlassen, als diese Hütte und den Weinberg, der daran stößt. Allein in diesem Weinberge liegt ein Schatz verborgen. Grabet fleißig nach, so werdet ihr ihn finden.

Nach dem Tode des Vaters gruben die Söhne den ganzen Weinberg mit dem größten Fleiße um, aber sie fanden weder Gold noch Silber. Da sie aber den Boden noch nie mit soviel Sorgfalt bearbeitet hatten, so brachte er eine solche Menge Trauben hervor, daß sie darüber erstaunten.

Jetzt erriethen die Söhne, was ihr Vater mit dem Schatze gemeint hatte, und sie schrieben an die Thür des Weinberges mit großen Buchstaben: Arbeitsamkeit ist der größte Schatz des Menschen.

5. *The oak and the willow.*

Nach einer sehr stürmischen Nacht ging ein Vater mit seinem Sohne auf das Feld, um zu sehen, welchen Schaden der Sturm verursacht habe. Sieh doch, rief der Knabe, da liegt die große, starke Eiche auf dem Boden hingestreckt, während die schwache Weide am Bache noch aufrecht dasteht. Ich hätte geglaubt, der Sturmwind würde leichter die Weide als die Eiche niedergerissen haben.

Mein Sohn, sagte der Vater, die stolze Eiche, die sich nicht biegen kann, mußte brechen; allein die geschmeidige Weide hat dem Sturmwinde nachgegeben und ist daher verschont geblieben.

6. *The grateful lion.*

Ein armer Sklave, der aus dem Hause seines Herrn entflohen war, wurde zum Tode verurtheilt. Man führte ihn auf einen großen Platz, welcher mit Mauern umgeben war, und ließ einen furchtbaren Löwen auf ihn los. Tausende von Menschen waren Zeugen dieses Schauspiels.

Der Löwe sprang grimmig auf den armen Menschen zu; allein plötzlich blieb er stehen, wedelte mit dem Schweife, hüpfte voll Freude um ihn herum und leckte ihm freundlich die Hände. Jedermann verwunderte sich und fragte den Sklaven, wie das komme.

Der Sklave erzählte: Als ich meinem Herrn entlaufen

war, verbarg ich mich in eine Höhle mitten in der Wüste. Da kam auf einmal dieser Löwe herein, winselte und zeigte mir seine Tatze, in der ein großer Dorn stack. Ich zog ihm den Dorn heraus und von der Zeit an versah mich der Löwe mit Wildpret und wir lebten in der Höhle friedlich zusammen. Bei der letzten Jagd wurden wir gefangen und voneinander getrennt. Nun freut sich das gute Thier, mich wieder gefunden zu haben.

Alles Volk war über die Dankbarkeit dieses wilden Thieres entzückt und bat laut um Gnade für den Sklaven und den Löwen. Der Sklave wurde frei gelassen und reichlich beschenkt. Der Löwe folgte ihm wie ein Hündchen und blieb stets bei ihm, ohne Jemand ein Leid zu thun.

Collection of words.

1. *The town.*

Die Stadt, the town;
die Vorstadt, the suburb;
das Thor, the gate;
der Platz, the square;
der Markt, the market-place;
die Straße, the street;
das Pflaster, the pavement;
das Haus, the house;
das Gebäude, the building;
die Kirche, the church;
der Thurm, the tower, spire;
die Domkirche, the cathedral;
die Post, the post-office;
das Zollhaus, the custom-house;
das Theater, the theatre;
die Börse, the exchange;
das Spital, the hospital;
das Wirthshaus, the inn;
das Kaffeehaus, the coffee-house;
der Palast, the palace;
die Mauer, the wall;
die Festung, the fortress;
der Hafen, the harbour;
die Umgegend, the environs.

2. *The house.*

Das Haus, the house;
die Thür, the door;
das Thor, the gate;
das Schloß, the lock;
der Schlüssel, the key;
die Klingel, the bell;
die Treppe, the staircase;
eine Stufe, a step;
ein Zimmer, a room;
der Saal, the saloon;
das Fenster, the window;
die Laden, the shutters;
die Decke, the ceiling,
der Fußboden, the floor;
die Wand, the wall;
der Kamin, the chimney;
die Küche, the kitchen;
der Keller, the cellar;
der Speicher, the garret, loft.
das Dach, the roof;
der Hof, the court-yard;
der Garten, the garden;
der Stall, the stable;
der Brunnen, the well.

3. *The furniture.*

Der Tisch, the table;
der Stuhl, the chair;
der Spiegel, the looking-glass;
der Schrank, the wardrobe;
die Kommode, the chest of drawers;
das Kanapee, the couch;
das Gemälde, the picture;

die Stanbuhr, the clock;
das Bett, the bed;
die Matratze, the mattress;
die Decke, the bed-cloth;
der Ofen, the stove;
der Leuchter, the candlestick;
der Löffel, the spoon;
die Gabel, the fork;
das Messer, the knife;
die Tasse, the cup and saucer;
das Tischtuch, the table-cloth;
das Tellertuch, the napkin;
das Handtuch, the towel;
die Lichtschere, the snuffers;
der Teller, the plate;
das Kissen, the pillow;
das Betttuch, the sheet;
die Vorhänge, the curtains;
das Glas, the glass;
die Flasche, the bottle;
der Korb, the basket.

4. *The professions.*

Das Handwerk, the profession;
der Handwerker, the artisan;
der Metzger, the butcher;
der Bäcker, the baker;
der Müller, the miller;
der Hutmacher, the hatter;
der Schneider, the tailor;
der Schuster, the shoemaker;
der Barbier, the barber;
der Schreiner, the joiner;
der Zimmermann, the carpenter;
der Glaser, the glazier;
der Schlosser, the lock smith;
der Schmied, the smith;
der Hufschmied, the farrier;
der Sattler, the saddler;
der Böttcher, the cooper;
der Gerber, the tanner;
der Kaufmann, the merchant;
der Buchhändler, the bookseller;
der Buchbinder, the bookbinder;
der Maurer, the mason;
die Näherin, the seamstress;
die Wäscherin, the laundress.

5. *The victuals.*

Das Brot, the bread;
das Mehl, the meal, flour;
das Fleisch, the meat;
der Braten, the roast-meat;
Kalbfleisch, veal;
Rindfleisch, beef;
Hammelfleisch, mutton;
der Fisch, the fish;
das Ei, the egg;
der Salat, the salad;
der Senf, the mustard;
das Salz, the salt;
das Oel, the oil;
der Essig, the vinegar;
Schweinefleisch, pork;
der Schinken, the ham;
das Gemüse, the vegetable;
die Suppe, the soup;
der Kohl, the cabbage;
die Kartoffel, the potato;
die Erbse, the pea;
die Bohne, the bean;
der Kuchen, the cake;
das Obst, the fruit;
der Pfeffer, the pepper;
die Butter, the butter;
der Käse, the cheese;
die Milch, the milk;

der Wein, the wine;
das Bier, the beer;
das Frühstück, the breakfast;
das Mittagsessen, the dinner;
das Vesperbrot, the afternoon's luncheon;
das Abendessen, the supper.

6. *The clothing.*

Der Rock, the coat;
das Kleid, the gown;
der Mantel, the cloak;
die Weste, the waistcoat;
die Jacke, the jacket;
der Schuh, the shoe;
der Strumpf, the stocking;
der Stiefel, the boot;
der Pantoffel, the slipper;
das Hemd, the shirt, shift;
die Schürze, the apron;
der Handschuh, the glove;
der Ring, the ring;
das Taschentuch, the handkerchief;
der Hut, the hat;
die Mütze, the cap;
die Uhr, the watch;
der Regenschirm, the umbrella;
der Sonnenschirm, the parasol;
der Fächer, the fan;
der Schleier, the veil;
der Stock, the cane;
der Beutel, the purse;
die Brille, the spectacles.

7. *The human body.*

Der Mensch, the man;
der Körper, the body;
der Kopf, the head;
das Haar, the hair;
das Gesicht, the face;
die Stirne, the forehead;
das Auge, the eye;
die Nase, the nose;
das Ohr, the ear;
der Mund, the mouth;
das Kinn, the chin;
der Bart, the beard;
die Lippe, the lip;
der Zahn, the tooth;
die Zunge, the tongue;
der Hals, the neck;
die Schulter, the shoulder;
der Rücken, the back;
der Arm, the arm;
die Hand, the hand;
der Finger, the finger;
der Nagel, the nail;
die Brust, the breast;
das Herz, the heart;
der Magen, the stomach;
das Bein, the leg;
der Fuß, the foot;
das Knie, the knee;
die Zehe, the toe;
das Gehirn, the brain.

8. *The quadrupeds.*

Das Thier, the animal;
das Pferd, the horse;
der Esel, the donkey;
der Hund, the dog;

die Katze, the cat;
die Ratte, the rat;
die Maus, the mouse;
der Maulwurf, the mole;
das Schwein, the pig;
die Ziege, the goat;
die Gemse, the chamois;
der Hase, the hare;
das Eichhorn, the squirrel;
der Affe, the monkey;
der Hirsch, the stag;
das Reh, the roe;

der Ochse, the ox;
der Stier, the bull;
die Kuh, the cow;
das Kalb, the calf;
das Schaf, the sheep;
das Lamm, the lamb;
der Fuchs, the fox;
der Wolf, the wolf;
der Bär, the bear;
der Löwe, the lion;
das Kameel, the camel;
der Elefant, the elephant.

9. *The birds.*

Der Vogel, the bird;
der Hahn, the cock;
das Huhn, the hen;
das Hühnchen, the chicken;
der Schwan, the swan;
die Gans, the goose;
die Ente, the duck;
die Taube, the pigeon;
der Pfau, the peacock;
die Wachtel, the quail;
die Schnepfe, the snipe;

das Rebhuhn, the partridge;
der Krammetsvogel, the fieldfare;
die Amsel, the black-bird;
die Lerche, the lark;
die Nachtigal, the nightingale;
die Schwalbe, the swallow;
der Zeisig, the green-finch;
der Fink, the finch;
der Sperling, the sparrow.

10. *The fishes and insects.*

Der Fisch, the fish;
der Hecht, the pike;
der Lachs, the salmon;
der Karpfen, the carp;
die Schleie, the tench;
der Aal, the eel;
die Forelle, the trout;
die Kröte, the toad;
der Frosch, the frog;
der Wurm, the worm;
die Raupe, the caterpillar;
die Ameise, the ant;

die Spinne, the spider;
der Häring, the herring;
die Auster, the oyster;
die Muschel, the muscle-fish
der Krebs, the craw-fish;
die Schlange, the snake;
die Fliege, the fly;
die Biene, the bee;
die Wespe, the wasp;
der Schmetterling, the butterfly.

11. *The trees and flowers.*

Der Baum, the tree;
der Apfelbaum, the apple-tree;
der Birnbaum, the pear-tree;
der Pflaumenbaum, the plum-tree;
der Kirschbaum, the cherry-tree;
der Nußbaum, the nut-tree;
die Eiche, the oak-tree;
die Fichte, the pine-tree;
die Tanne, the fir-tree;
die Buche, the beech;
die Ulme, the elm;
die Pappel, the poplar;
die Blume, the flower;
die Rose, the rose;
die Nelke, the pink;
die Tulpe, the tulip;
die Lilie, the lily;
die Levkoje, the stock;
das Veilchen, the violet;
die Maiblume, the lily of the valley;
die Kornblume, the corn flower;
der Flieder, the lilac;
die Sonnenblume, the sunflower;
das Geisblatt, the honeysuckle.

12. *The country.*

Das Land, the country, land;
das Feld, the field;
die Gegend, the country;
die Ebene, the plain;
der Berg, the mountain;
das Thal, the valley;
der Wald, the forest;
der Busch, the copse;
der Weg, the road;
der Bach, the brook;
die Wiese, the meadow;
die Haide, the heath;
der Hügel, the hill;
die Hütte, the cottage;
das Dorf, the village;
der Flecken, the borough;
das Schloß, the castle;
der Meierhof, the farm;
die Mühle, the mill;
das Korn, the corn;
der Weizen, the wheat;
die Gerste, the barley;
der Hafer, the oats;
das Stroh, the straw;
das Heu, the hay;
die Traube, the bunch of grapes

Easy dialogues.

1.

Eating and drinking.

Are you hungry?	Sind Sie hungerig?
I have a good appetite.	Ich habe guten Appetit.
I am very hungry.	Ich bin sehr hungerig.
Eat something.	Essen Sie etwas.
What will you eat?	Was wollen Sie essen?
What do you wish to eat?	Was wünschen Sie zu essen?
You do not eat.	Sie essen nicht.
I beg your pardon; I eat very heartily.	Ich bitte um Verzeihung, ich esse sehr viel.
I have eaten very heartily.	Ich habe sehr viel gegessen.
I have dined with a good appetite.	Ich habe mit gutem Appetit zu Mittag gegessen.
Eat another piece.	Essen Sie noch ein Stückchen.
I can eat no more.	Ich kann nichts mehr genießen.
Are you thirsty?	Sind Sie durstig?
Are you not thirsty?	Haben Sie keinen Durst?
I am very thirsty.	Ich bin sehr durstig.
I am dying of thirst.	Ich vergehe vor Durst.
Let us drink.	Lassen Sie uns trinken.
Give me something to drink.	Geben Sie mir zu trinken.
Will you drink a glass of wine?	Wollen Sie ein Glas Wein trinken?
Drink a glass of beer.	Trinken Sie ein Glas Bier.
Drink another glass of wine.	Trinken Sie noch ein Glas Wein.
Sir, I drink to your health.	Mein Herr, ich trinke auf Ihre Gesundheit.
have the honor to drink to your health.	Ich habe die Ehre, auf Ihre Gesundheit zu trinken.

2.

Going and coming.

Where are you going?	Wohin gehen Sie?
I am going home.	Ich gehe nach Hause.
I was going to your house.	Ich wollte zu Ihnen.
Where do you come from?	Woher kommen Sie?
I come from my brother's.	Ich komme von meinem Bruder.
I am coming from church.	Ich komme aus der Kirche.
I just left the school.	Ich komme soeben aus der Schule.
Will you go with me?	Wollen Sie mit mir gehen?
Whither do you wish to go?	Wohin wollen Sie gehen?
We will go for a walk.	Wir wollen spazierengehen.
We will take a walk.	Wir wollen einen Spaziergang machen.
With all my heart, most willingly.	Sehr gern, mit Vergnügen.
What way shall we take?	Welchen Weg wollen wir nehmen?
Any way you like.	Welchen Weg Sie wollen.
Let us go into the park.	Lassen Sie uns in den Park gehen.
Let us take your friend in our way.	Lassen Sie uns im Vorbeigehen Ihren Freund abholen.
As you please.	Wie es Ihnen gefällig ist.
Is Mr. B. at home?	Ist Herr B. zu Hause?
He is gone out.	Er ist ausgegangen.
He is not at home.	Er ist nicht zu Hause.
Can you tell us where he is gone?	Können Sie uns sagen, wohin er gegangen ist?
I cannot tell you precisely.	Ich kann es Ihnen nicht gewiß sagen.
I think he is gone to see his sister.	Ich glaube, daß er zu seiner Schwester gegangen ist.
Do you know when he will come back?	Wissen Sie, wann er zurückkommt?
No he said nothing of it; when he went out.	Nein; er hat nichts davon gesagt, als er ging.
Then we must go without him	Dann müssen wir ohne ihn gehen.

3.

Questions and answers.

Come nearer; I have something to tell you.	Treten Sie näher, ich habe Ihnen etwas zu sagen.
I have a word to say to you.	Ich habe Ihnen ein Wörtchen zu sagen.
Listen to me.	Hören Sie mich an.
I want to speak to you.	Ich möchte mit Ihnen sprechen.
What is at your service?	Was steht zu Ihren Diensten?
I am speaking to you.	Ich spreche mit Ihnen.
I am not speaking to you.	Ich spreche nicht mit Ihnen.
What do you say?	Was sagen Sie?
What did you say?	Was haben Sie gesagt?
I say nothing.	Ich sage nichts.
Do you hear?	Hören Sie?
Do you hear what I say?	Verstehen Sie, was ich sage?
Do you understand me?	Verstehen Sie mich?
Will you be so kind as to repeat....?	Wollen Sie so gut sein, zu wiederholen....?
I understand you well.	Ich verstehe Sie wohl.
Why do you not answer me?	Warum antworten Sie mir nicht?
Do you not speak French?	Sprechen Sie nicht Französisch?
Very little, Sir.	Sehr wenig, mein Herr.
I understand it a little, but I do not speak it.	Ich verstehe es ein wenig, aber ich spreche es nicht.
Speak louder.	Sprechen Sie lauter.
Do not speak so loud.	Sprechen Sie nicht so laut.
Do not make so much noise.	Machen Sie nicht soviel Lärm.
Hold your tongue.	Schweigen Sie.
Did you not tell me that...?	Sagten Sie mir nicht, daß...?
Who told you that?	Wer hat Ihnen das gesagt?
They have told me so.	Man hat es mir gesagt.
Somebody has told it me.	Es hat mir's Jemand gesagt.
I have heard it.	Ich habe es gehört.
What do you wish to say?	Was wollen Sie sagen?
What is that good for?	Wozu soll das dienen?
How do you call that?	Wie nennen Sie das?
That is called....	Das heißt....
May I ask you....?	Darf ich Sie fragen....?
What do you wish?	Was wünschen Sie?

Do you know Mr. G.?	Kennen Sie Herrn G.?
I know him by sight.	Ich kenne ihn von Ansehen.
I know him by name.	Ich kenne ihn dem Namen nach

4.
The age.

How old are you?	Wie alt sind Sie?
How old is your brother?	Wie alt ist Ihr Herr Bruder?
I am twelve years old.	Ich bin zwölf Jahre alt.
I am ten years and six months old.	Ich bin zehn und ein halbes Jahr alt.
Next month I shall be sixteen years old.	Im nächsten Monat werde ich sechzehn Jahr alt.
I was eighteen years old last week.	Vergangene Woche bin ich achtzehn Jahre alt geworden.
You do not look so old.	Sie sehen nicht so alt aus.
You look older.	Sie sehen älter aus.
I thought you were older.	Ich hielt Sie für älter.
I did not think you were so old.	Ich hielt Sie nicht für so alt.
How old may your uncle be?	Wie alt mag Ihr Oheim sein?
He may be sixty years old.	Er kann etwa sechzig Jahre haben.
He is about sixty years old.	Er ist ungefähr sechzig Jahre alt.
He is more than fifty years old.	Er ist über funfzig Jahre alt.
He is a man of fifty and upwards.	Er ist ein Mann von funfzig und einigen Jahren.
He may be sixty or thereabouts.	Er kann etwa sechzig Jahre zählen.
He is above eighty.	Er ist über achtzig Jahre.
That is a great age.	Das ist ein hohes Alter.
Is he so old?	Ist er so alt?
He begins to grow old.	Er fängt an zu altern.

5.
The time.

What o'clock is it?	Wie viel Uhr ist es?
Pray tell me what time it is.	Ich bitte, sagen Sie mir, welche Zeit es ist

It is one o'clock.	Es ist ein Uhr.
It is past one.	Es ist ein Uhr vorbei.
It has struck one.	Es hat eins geschlagen.
It is a quarter past one.	Es ist ein Viertel auf zwei.
It is half past one.	Es ist halb zwei.
It wants ten minutes to two.	Es fehlen zehn Minuten an zwei.
It is not yet two o'clock.	Es ist noch nicht zwei Uhr.
It is only twelve o'clock.	Es ist erst zwölf.
It is almost three o'clock.	Es ist beinahe drei.
It is on the stroke of three.	Es ist gegen drei.
It is going to strike three.	Es wird gleich drei Uhr schlagen.
It is ten minutes past three.	Es ist zehn Minuten nach drei.
The clock is going to strike.	Die Uhr wird sogleich schlagen.
There the clock strikes.	Da schlägt die Uhr.
It is not late.	Es ist nicht spät.
It is later than I thought.	Es ist später als ich dachte.
I did not think it was so late.	Ich dachte nicht, daß es so spät wäre.

6.

The weather.

What kind of weather is it?	Was ist es für Wetter?
It is bad weather.	Es ist schlechtes Wetter.
It is very cloudy.	Es ist trübe.
It is dreadful weather.	Es ist ein abscheuliches Wetter.
It is fine weather.	Es ist schönes Wetter.
We are going to have a fine day.	Wir werden einen schönen Tag haben.
It is dewy.	Es thaut.
It is foggy.	Es ist nebelig.
It is rainy weather.	Es ist regnerisches Wetter.
It threatens to rain.	Es droht zu regnen.
The sky becomes very cloudy.	Der Himmel umzieht sich.
The sky is getting very dark.	Der Himmel wird dunkel.
The sun is coming out.	Die Sonne fängt an sich zu zeigen.
The weather is clearing up again.	Das Wetter klärt sich wieder auf.
It is very hot.	Es ist sehr heiß.

It is moon-light.	Der Mond scheint.
Do you think it will be fine weather?	Glauben Sie, daß es gutes Wetter geben wird?
I do not think that it will rain.	Ich glaube nicht, daß es regnen wird.
I am afraid it will rain.	Ich fürchte, es wird regnen.
I fear so.	Ich fürchte es.

7.
The salutation.

Good morning, Sir!	Guten Morgen, mein Herr!
I wish you a good morning.	Ich wünsche Ihnen guten Morgen.
How do you do?	Wie befinden Sie sich?
How is your health?	Wie geht es mit Ihrer Gesundheit?
Do you continue in good health?	Befinden Sie sich immer wohl?
Pretty good; and how is yours?	Ziemlich wohl, und Sie?
Do I see you well?	Sind Sie wohl?
Very well, and you?	Sehr wohl, und Sie auch?
I am perfectly well.	Ich befinde mich sehr wohl.
And how is it with you?	Und wie geht es Ihnen?
As usual.	Wie gewöhnlich.
Pretty well, thank God.	Ziemlich gut, Gott sei Dank.
I am very happy to see you well.	Es freut mich sehr, Sie wohl zu sehen.

8.
The visit.

There is a knock.	Es klopft.
Somebody knocks.	Es klopft Jemand.
Go and see who it is.	Geh' und sieh, wer da ist.
Go and open the door.	Geh' und öffne die Thür.
It is Mrs. B.	Es ist Madame B.
I wish you a good morning.	Ich wünsche Ihnen guten Morgen.
I am happy to see you.	Es freut mich, Sie zu sehen.
I have not seen you this age.	Es ist ein Jahrhundert, seit ich Sie nicht sah.

Ahn. Method. I.

It is a novelty to see you.	Es ist eine Seltenheit, Sie zu sehen.
Pray, sit down.	Setzen Sie sich, ich bitte.
Sit down, if you please.	Setzen Sie sich gefälligst.
Take a seat.	Nehmen Sie Platz.
Give a chair to the lady.	Gib Madame einen Stuhl.
Will you stay and take some dinner with us?	Wollen Sie zum Mittagsessen bei uns bleiben?
I cannot stay.	Ich kann nicht bleiben.
I only came in to see how you are.	Ich bin nur gekommen, um zu erfahren, wie Sie sich befinden.
I must go.	Ich muß gehen.
You are in a great hurry.	Sie sind sehr eilig.
Why are you in such a hurry?	Weshalb sind Sie so eilig?
I have a great many things to do.	Ich habe viel zu thun.
Surely, you can stay a little longer.	Sie können wol noch einen Augenblick bleiben.
I will stay longer another time.	Ein ander mal will ich länger bleiben.
I thank you for your visit.	Ich danke Ihnen für Ihren Besuch.
I hope to see you soon again.	Ich hoffe Sie bald wieder zu sehen.

9.
Breakfast.

Have you breakfasted?	Haben Sie gefrühstückt?
Not yet.	Noch nicht.
You are come just in time.	Sie kommen gerade zu rechter Zeit.
You will breakfast with us.	Sie werden mit uns frühstücken.
Breakfast is ready.	Das Frühstück ist bereit.
Do you drink tea or coffee?	Trinken Sie Thee oder Kaffee?
Would you prefer chocolate?	Wollen Sie vielleicht lieber Chokolade?
I prefer coffee.	Ich ziehe den Kaffee vor.
What can I offer you?	Was kann ich Ihnen anbieten?

Here are rolls and toast.	Hier sind Milchbrötchen und geröstete Brotschnittchen.
What do you like best?	Was mögen Sie am liebsten?
I shall take a roll.	Ich werde ein Brötchen nehmen.
How do you like the coffee?	Wie finden Sie den Kaffee?
Is the coffee strong enough?	Ist der Kaffee stark genug?
It is excellent.	Er ist vortrefflich.
Is there enough sugar in it?	Ist genug Zucker darin?
If there is not, do not make any ceremony.	Ist es nicht, so machen Sie keine Complimente.
Do as if you were at home.	Thun Sie, als ob Sie zu Hause wären.

10.
Before dinner.

At what time do we dine to-day?	Um welche Zeit essen wir heute zu Mittag?
We shall dine at two o'clock.	Wir werden um zwei Uhr essen.
We shall not dine before three o'clock.	Wir werden nicht vor drei Uhr essen.
Shall we have anybody at dinner to-day?	Werden wir heute zum Essen Jemanden bei uns haben?
Do you expect company?	Erwarten Sie Gesellschaft?
I expect Mr. B.	Ich erwarte Herrn B.
Mr. D. has promised to come if the weather permits it.	Herr D. hat versprochen, zu kommen, wenn es das Wetter erlaubt.
Have you given orders for dinner?	Haben Sie die Befehle zum Mittagsessen gegeben?
What have you ordered for dinner?	Was haben Sie zum Essen bestellt?
Have you sent for fish?	Haben Sie Fisch besorgen lassen?
I could not get any fish.	Ich habe keinen Fisch bekommen können.
I fear we shall have a very indifferent dinner.	Ich besorge, daß wir kein sonderliches Mittagsessen haben werden.
We must do as we can.	Wir müssen uns behelfen.

11.

Dinner.

What shall I help you to?	Was soll ich Ihnen vorlegen?
Will you take a little soup?	Wollen Sie etwas Suppe?
No, I thank you. I will trouble you for a little beef.	Ich danke. Ich werde Sie um etwas Rindfleisch bitten.
It looks so very nice.	Es sieht so gut aus.
Which piece do you like best?	Welches Stück haben Sie am liebsten?
I hope this piece is to your liking.	Ich hoffe, daß dies Stück nach Ihrem Geschmacke ist.
Gentlemen, you have dishes near you.	Meine Herren, die Schüsseln stehen vor Ihnen.
Help yourselves.	Bedienen Sie sich.
Take without ceremony what you like best.	Nehmen Sie ohne Umstände, was Ihnen beliebt.
Would you like a little of this roast-meat?	Wollen Sie ein wenig von diesem Braten?
Do you take fat?	Wollen Sie Fettes?
Give me some of this lean, if you please.	Geben Sie mir Mageres, wenn es Ihnen gefällig ist.
How do you like the roast-meat?	Wie finden Sie den Braten?
It is excellent, delicious.	Er ist vortrefflich, köstlich.
What will you take with your meat?	Was wünschen Sie zum Fleisch?
May I help you to some vegetables?	Darf ich Ihnen Gemüse geben?
Will you take peas or cauliflower?	Wünschen Sie Erbsen oder Blumenkohl?
It is quite indifferent to me.	Es ist mir ganz gleich.
I shall send you a piece of this fowl.	Ich will Ihnen ein Stückchen von diesem Geflügel reichen.
No, thank you, I can eat no more.	Ich danke, ich kann nichts mehr essen.
You are a poor eater.	Sie sind ein schwacher Esser.
You eat nothing.	Sie essen gar nichts.
I beg your pardon, I do honour to your dinner.	Ich bitte um Verzeihung, ich mache Ihrem Essen Ehre.
You may take away.	Ihr könnt alsbann abbeden.

12.

Tea.

Have you carried in the tea-things?	Hast du Alles gebracht, was zum Thee gehört?
Everything is on the table.	Es ist Alles auf dem Tische.
Does the water boil?	Kocht das Wasser?
Tea is ready.	Der Thee ist fertig.
They are waiting for you.	Sie werden erwartet.
Here I am.	Hier bin ich.
We have not cups enough.	Wir haben nicht Tassen genug.
We want two more cups and saucers.	Wir müssen noch zwei Tassen haben.
Bring another tea-spoon and a saucer.	Bringe noch einen Theelöffel und eine Untertasse.
You have not brought in the sugar-tongs.	Du hast die Zuckerzange nicht gebracht.
Do you take cream?	Nehmen Sie Rahm?
The tea is so strong.	Der Thee ist so stark.
I shall thank you for a little more milk.	Ich werde noch um etwas Milch bitten.
Here are cakes and muffins.	Hier ist Kuchen und Brotkuchen.
Do you prefer some bread and butter?	Essen Sie lieber Butterbrot?
I shall take a slice of bread and butter.	Ich werde ein Butterbrot nehmen.
Pass the plate this way.	Schieb den Teller hierher.
Ring the bell, if you please.	Schellen Sie gefälligst.
Will you kindly ring the bell?	Wollen Sie gütigst die Klingel ziehen?
We want some more water.	Wir brauchen noch mehr Wasser.
Bring it as quickly as possible.	Bringe es so schnell als möglich.
Make haste.	Beeile dich.
Take the plate with you.	Nimm den Teller mit.
Is your tea sweet enough?	Ist Ihr Thee süß genug?
Have I put sugar enough in your tea?	Habe ich genug Zucker in Ihren Thee gethan?
It is excellent.	Er ist vortrefflich.
I do not like it quite so sweet.	Ich habe ihn nicht gern so süß.
Your tea is very good.	Ihr Thee ist sehr gut.

Where do you buy it?	Wo kaufen Sie ihn?
I buy it at....	Ich kaufe ihn bei....
Have you already done?	Sind Sie schon fertig?
You will take another cup.	Sie werden noch eine Tasse nehmen.
I shall pour you out half a cup.	Ich werde Ihnen noch eine halbe Tasse einschenken.
You will not refuse me.	Sie werden es mir nicht abschlagen.
I have already drunk three cups, and I never drink more.	Ich habe schon drei Tassen getrunken, und mehr trinke ich nie.